Safety Metrics

Tools and Techniques for Measuring Safety Performance

Christopher A. Janicak, Ph.D., CSP, ARM
Associate Professor of Safety
Department of Safety Sciences
Indiana University of Pennsylvania

Government Institutes
An imprint of
The Scarecrow Press, Inc.
Lanham, Maryland • Toronto • Oxford

 **Government Institutes**

Published in the United States of America
by Government Institutes, an imprint of The Scarecrow Press, Inc.
A wholly owned subsidiary of
The Rowman & Littlefield Publishing Group, Inc.
4501 Forbes Boulevard, Suite 200
Lanham, Maryland 20706
http://govinst.scarecrowpress.com

PO Box 317
Oxford
OX2 9RU, UK

British Library Cataloguing in Publication Information Available

Library of Congress Cataloging-in-Publication Data

Janicak, Christopher A.
  Safety metrics : tools and techniques for measuring safety performance /
  Christopher A. Janicak.
      p. cm.
  Includes bibliographical references and index.
  ISBN 0-86587-947-8
    1. Industrial safety—Evaluation—Statistical methods. 2. Industrial
management—Evaluation—Statistical methods. I. Title.
T55.3.S72 J63 2002
620.8'6—dc21   2002033912

To my wife, Nancy, and son, Justin.

Summary Contents

Contents

1
Safety Performance Programs 1

2
Safety Performance Measurement 7

3
Statistical Methods in Safety Metrics 19

4
Run Charts and Control Charts.....................43

5
Trending and Forecasting 75

6

Effective Data Presentation 85

7

Establishing a Safety Metrics Program 93

8

Benchmarking 99

9

Auditing Safety Performance 105

10
Insurance Rating Systems 113

11
Behavior-Based Safety Metrics 119

12
Evaluating Safety Training 125

13
Assessing the Safety Climate 133

14
Performance Indices 141

15
Voluntary Performance Standards 151

List of Figures and Tables

Introduction

Safety metrics is a system of tools and techniques that allows safety managers to measure safety performance with the same quantitative precision as other indicators of an organization's productivity. An effective safety metrics program begins with the proper planning and a management structure. This program includes the identification of the indicators of a successful safety program. The goal of this book is to present, in an understandable and practical manner, the tools and techniques needed to put this program into action.

When safety professionals first began using safety metrics, they routinely measured safety performance in terms of accidents and losses. However, over the years, as the safety profession has become more sophisticated, so also have the techniques used to measure its execution. A successful program should include combinations of various types of performance measures. As with any data collection, the safety professional must also keep in mind the validity and reliability of the performance measures. Only with accurate and consistent data can the proper conclusions be reached, and the necessary control strategies implemented.

The main focus for a safety metrics program is the identification of gaps or deficiencies in the data obtained versus the desired outcome as established in the program goals or benchmarks. Identification of these deficiencies can be readily achieved through the use of control charts and various statistical techniques. Depending upon the data collected, the appropriate charts can be constructed and trends identified. Finally, a growing trend in safety management is the focus on the elimination of unsafe acts and behaviors. Rather than waiting for accidents and losses to occur, a proactive approach of monitoring unsafe behaviors and than addressing them has become an integral part of a safety performance program.

This book provides safety practitioners with information and tools that can be used to develop and implement a safety metrics program. Techniques are presented to assist the safety professional in implementing a safety metrics program, establishing performance measures, analyzing data, and determining the need for corrective action.

About the Author

Chistopher A. Janicak is an Associate Professor of Safety at Indiana University of Pennsylvania's Department of Safety Sciences. He holds a Doctor of Philosophy degree in Research Methodology, a Master of Science degree in Industrial Technology with an Industrial Safety concentration, and a Bachelor of Science degree in Health and Safety Studies with an Occupational Safety and Health Education concentration. He is published widely in professional journals, including the *The Journal of Safety Research* and *Professional Safety*. Dr. Janicak is a professional member of the American Society of Safety Engineers (ASSE).

Christopher A. Janicak, Ph.D., CSP, ARM
Associate Professor of Safety
Department of Safety Sciences
Indiana University of Pennsylvania
Indiana, PA 15705-1087
Telephone: 724-357-3018
Fax: 724-357-3992
Email: cjanicak@iup.edu

Safety Performance Programs

Safety professionals must be able to determine if their programs are making a positive impact upon the organization, confirm whether they are meeting their safety goals, and communicate the status of the safety performance to the organization. In order to verify the improvement of workplace safety, safety professionals rely upon measures they believe to be indicative of performance. There can be wide differences in how these measures work, how they tie into an organization's safety activities, and how they are used to institute change in the organization. Historically, safety practitioners have often chosen ineffective, inadequate, and invalid measures (Petersen 1998). Some of these more traditional, and less exact, forms of safety performance measures include the number of lost workdays, the number of injuries, and financial losses. To avoid the shortcomings of these overly simplistic measures, safety metrics must be based upon sound business practices and statistical procedures, and should be used to implement a process of measuring safety programs.

The steps involved in a safety metrics program include program development, benchmarking, auditing, measuring performance, evaluating outcomes, and managing the program based upon the outcomes. A successful safety metrics program requires accountability, a management structure, and a data collection system. The basic method of the program is to systematically gather data and analyze it to determine whether the organization's performance goals have been met. Analysis may include comparisons to established benchmarks, goals, or other collected data.

The final key component of any safety performance program is the follow-up. Follow-up should be based on the trends and differences identified in the analysis. It can include developing new policies and procedures, modifying existing policies and procedures, or changing the physical characteristics of the workplace or job task.

Definition of Safety Metrics

The term "safety metrics" refers to the body of knowledge used to quantify and measure safety performance. *A safety metric is the measurement of key processes in order to provide an objective basis for determining process performance* (Daugherty 1999, 144). On the corporate level, metrics identifies divisions or facilities that need to improve within the safety process. At the plant level, metrics identifies departments and work areas that need to improve.

An underlying premise of safety metrics is continual performance improvement. The recent Total Quality Management (TQM) movement and its emphasis on continual improvement has increased the popularity and ease of implementing formalized safety metrics programs, especially since performance measures are generally recognized as an important element of all TQM programs (TRADE 1995, 1-3). By applying the same underlying principles to safety metrics, and through focusing on specifics and sustained employee involvement, safety professionals can use safety metrics as a valuable tool for improving overall safety performance.

Safety Performance Measures

While safety metrics is used to quantify or describe the organization's safety performance, performance measurement consists of determining what to measure, identifying data collection methods, and collecting the data. Safety performance measures are indicators that focus on the differences between actual safety performance and what has been defined as acceptable. Performance measures are tools employees and management can use to continually guide and calculate their own improvement by regularly measuring individual, team, and site-wide performance. The performance measures identify problem areas, provide some measure of accountability for employees, and corroborate the fact that the organization's goals are (or are not) being met. A performance measure can be used to motivate managers and employees, to monitor important activities, and to help evaluate whether those activities need revision to achieve organizational strategies. An important aspect of any safety metrics program is the link between performance measures and the desired outcome. Performance measures assess the progress toward achieving a desired outcome, usually through explaining the causal relationships that exist between program activities and the outcome.

The ability to accurately measure safety performance depends heavily upon the process that is followed to quantify that performance. The quantification of performance should be done through the following systematic approach:

1. Define the standardized units of measure.
2. Develop instruments and methods that are capable of measuring in terms of the units of measure.
3. Use the instruments or methods to measure performance.

Safety Metrics Techniques

The safety professional has many tools and techniques available to establish a safety metrics program, collect data, evaluate performance, and make decisions based on the findings. Many of the tools and techniques presented in this book are commonly used in the quality management and productivity fields. Safety performance lends itself readily to these management tools. However, it has only been over the past decade or so that the safety profession has begun to use them with any regularity.

Data analysis tools and statistics are essential in the collection and evaluation of quantitative performance measures. While control charts have been used to graphically display and evaluate loss and accident information for years, more sophisticated control chart techniques and Pareto diagrams have been used only to a limited extent in the field. Yet by assessing safety data through descriptive and inferential statistics, a degree of statistical significance, and thus a higher level of certainty, can be added to the results. In addition, cause and effect analyses can be beneficial in identifying and evaluating the effectiveness of control measures. Through the use of these techniques, the safety professional can direct the organization's safety resources toward those areas that will have an impact on the organization's overall safety performance.

Current Trends in Safety Metrics

For years, measuring safety performance has meant solely counting the number of people hurt or the number of days away from work. This translates to after-the-fact hazard detection, which (like outdated quality programs based on inspecting defects at the end of a process) does not identify organizational errors—the true causes of accidents. "Safety excellence requires daily proactive intervention by line managers and supervisors. This proactive intervention is usually a missing link that can only be corrected when the system holds managers, supervisors, and executives accountable" (Petersen 2000, 19).

Today's safety professional has moved beyond the standard measurement of safety performance in terms of the number of accidents or injuries and recordable injury and illness rates. More sophisticated techniques that involve safety performance measurement systems, ongoing tracking of results, and continual improvement processes have replaced the early measurements. While today's safety metrics still include accident and illness performance, they also encompass behavior-based safety, safety program implementation performance, and insurance costs and losses.

Safety performance is now measured with the same tools and techniques common to quality measures of other aspects in the organization. Control charts, run charts, and Pareto diagrams can be used to track and monitor safety performance, establish trends, and evaluate program performance against accepted tolerances. Benchmarking against other high performers has become a trend in industry not only for production goals but also for safety.

In today's global economy, safety performance and its measurement have also become global. The International Organization for Standardization's ISO standards have become an integral part of many organizations' safety management philosophy. ISO

9000 and 14000 standards are global frameworks for many industries' quality and environmental performance standards. These standards have become the means by which organizations have incorporated safety into production and management strategies.

In Europe, the European Community has adopted a number of performance standards that serve as voluntary quality and environmental standards for its members. The European Foundation for Quality Management (EFQM) promotes and rewards organizations that adhere to their excellence model for quality. Accompanying these standards are safety and environmental performance measures that directly impact the overall quality of the product. These standards have also laid the foundation for documentation of performance standards and continual improvement process.

Summary

The safety professional has long been faced with trying to answer the question "How are we performing with regard to safety?" Tools and techniques that are often used in fields as diverse as business management, insurance, and psychology can also be applied to industrial safety. This book provides a framework for developing a management program designed to apply these techniques and identify activities that can be used to continually improve safety performance. Information contained in this book will provide the safety professional with:

1. Organizational frameworks that can be used to establish a safety performance improvement program
2. Benchmarking and safety goal-setting strategies
3. Different types of safety metrics that can be used to measure safety performance
4. Techniques for data collection, analysis, and presentation of performance measures.

Chapter Questions

1. Provide examples of three different measures that are commonly used to measure safety performance.
2. Historically, how well have the performance measures safety professionals selected measured performance?
3. What is safety metrics?
4. What is a safety metrics program?
5. Describe the safety metrics process.
6. What is the underlying premise of a safety metrics program?
7. Define performance measures.

8. An approach to quantifying performance measures should include what?
9. What purpose does data analysis and statistics serve with regards to measuring safety performance?
10. Describe the current trends in use for measuring safety performance in the workplace.

Safety Performance Measurement

Safety performance measures provide data indicating the status of safety activities (Training Resources and Data Exchange (TRADE) 1995, 1-36). Comparisons between performance measures and benchmarks or organizational goals allow the safety manager to make decisions and take appropriate action. The key difference between performance measures and safety metrics is that performance measures evaluate the safety process, and safety metrics are the standards of measurement (such as accident rates). A series of safety metrics makes up a safety performance measure.

One of the main advantages of using performance measures is that they enable companies to express the results of a safety process in quantitative, not qualitative, terms that can then be analyzed to determine efficiency of safety and health processes (Leandri 2001, 39). These measurements permit identification and prioritization. They also identify the most rewarding efforts and allow prioritization of company-wide issues.

A safety performance measurement system based upon continuous improvement processes requires the safety manager to have a program framework in place. This program framework, at a minimum, consists of defining acceptable levels of performance, collecting data, comparing performance against the acceptable levels, and finally, taking corrective action to improve performance levels. Development of this safety performance measurement system requires input from a variety of sources—both internal and external. Examples of internal input include management, engineering, production, and human resources. External sources of input can include other companies and professional organizations.

A framework assists in the development of a safety performance measurement program by establishing well-defined performance measures, identifying all areas of safety performance, and documenting procedures for implementing the program.

Performance Measure Framework

A suggested methodology for implementing performance measures can be established following the development of three tiers consisting of: 1) Mission and Vision,

2) Safety Objectives, and 3) Performance Measures (United States Department of Energy, Hanford Site 2001).

A mission statement communicates the broad goals and the organization's commitment to safety, to employees, and to the public. A common theme found in safety policy statements is that of ongoing safety performance assessment and improvement. It is through the safety policy statement that an organization establishes the safety climate.

An alternative framework for thinking about and creating performance measures is to divide them into three categories: key objectives, outcome measures, and activity measures (Leandri 2001, 39).

1) **Key objectives** are goals that say what a company expects from the safety program. They are big company goals that are inspirational and motivational in nature. Key objectives can be the organization's overall safety mission.

2) **Outcome measures** reflect the company's key safety objectives and are used to determine whether the company has reached them. These measures, sometimes referred to as "lagging" indicators, typically demonstrate the final results of the safety process. They are often commonly recognized or standard measures, such as those quoted in benchmarking studies. They are also the measures that tend to be tracked by CEOs, presidents, and vice presidents. Examples of outcome measures for a safety metrics program include lost workday rates, recordable injury rates, and number of miles driven without an accident. These indicators are referred to as "lagging" because they measure safety performances that are the result of, or occur after, an activity.

Activity → Outcome → Measure

3) **Activity measures** monitor the performance of activities that are needed to reach key objectives. They reflect focused safety issues such as the number of hazard surveys conducted, the number of employees trained in lockout/tagout procedures, etc. These measures, sometimes called "leading" indicators, typically demonstrate the state of work-in-progress in terms of cost, quality, and time. Often they are found in official internal reports and are likely to be tracked by directors, managers, and supervisors. Leading indicators are measures of the activity prior to the outcome.

Activity → Measure → Outcome

The Performance Measurement Process

The basic concept of performance measurement involves (a) planning and meeting established operating goals/standards, (b) detecting deviations from planned levels of performance, and (c) restoring performance to the planned levels or achieving new levels of performance.

The first requirement of a safety performance measure is a team approach to developing and implementing the program because safety and its improvement is not the responsibility of one department or one person but of everyone in the organization. Input from a variety of departments and employees is essential in developing a comprehensive program that includes all aspects of the organization. Involving groups of people also helps gain support for implementation of the program. A collaborative approach makes it easier to assess safety performance using safety metrics from various departments. For example, to measure safety performance with regard to back injuries, an organization can use a safety metric of recordable injuries from the personnel department, records of near miss incidents from the production department, and the number of visits to the plant emergency room from the medical department. In this situation, three departments have three different methods of measuring back injuries. This combined measurement provides a more accurate picture of the overall back injury prevention performance in the workplace. (If, for example, management looked only at the number of recordable injuries, and not at the number of near misses, they might be led to believe the workplace is safer than it is.)

The performance measurement process that one can follow can be separated into 11 discrete steps (Training Resources and Data Exchange (TRADE) 1995, 1-9–1-10). This framework describes the process generically and is intended to serve only as a guideline. The framework can be modified to meet the organization's needs. Steps in the process may be added, modified, or removed depending upon the organizational needs. It may be necessary to make these changes in the planning stages or as deemed necessary once the process is in place and feedback indicates that changes are necessary. An illustration of these process steps is provided in the following sections:

Suppose a water bottling company has been experiencing an increased frequency of back injuries and wishes to implement a safety performance measurement process.

1. Identify the process flow.
   First, the process is analyzed and broken down into its various job tasks. Workers are required to lift filled 5-gallon water bottles off of a conveyor, carry them, and place the bottles on pallets.

2. Identify Critical Activities To Be Measured.
   In this step, identify those aspects of the job tasks that can be measured in terms of safety performance. Examples of critical activity related to potential back injuries could be the lifting of the water bottles, moving filled pallets, etc. Examples of measurable outcomes related to back injury prevention include the number of bottles lifted using proper lifting techniques, the number of pallets moved using appropriate material handling devices, attendance at back injury prevention training programs, etc.

3. Establish Performance Goals or Standards.
   An example of a performance goal may be the reduction of recordable back injuries by 80 percent in a three-month period. The performance goals and standards

should include the measurable activity, the level to which acceptability is met, and the time period by which the goal should be attained.

4. Establish Performance Measurements.

   Individual performance measures should be defined that are indicative of the established performance goals. For example, with a goal of reducing back injuries, activities that can be measured include use of proper lifting techniques, providing and attending safety training related to back injury prevention, etc. The key is to establish measures that are tied to the performance goals and standards.

5. Identify Responsible Parties.

   Determine who will be responsible for implementing the safety performance program and establish methods of accountability.

6. Collect Data.

   Data needs should be identified, as well as the procedures for collection. The data requirements are identified through the established performance measures. Examples of data can include accident reports, job observations, training records, etc.

7. Data Analysis.

   The performance measure data requires analysis. The analysis techniques are tied to the performance measures and the performance goals. The format of the performance measures indicates the types of data analysis techniques that can or cannot be used (see Chapter 3). The performance goals are also tied to the analysis techniques. If the performance goal is the reduction of back injuries over a period of time, the analysis technique used should be capable of identifying such a decrease, if it does exist. (See Chapters 3 and 4 for a discussion of analysis techniques.)

8. Compare Actual Performance to Goals.

   With the data collected and analyzed, a comparison is made between the performance and the established goals. The safety manager ascertains differences between the obtained performance and the desired performance as defined by the performance goals.

9. Corrective Action.

   A decision is made at this point as to whether corrective action is necessary. If the performance levels fall short of the desired performance goals, further analysis as to the reasons for the results is necessary.

10. Make Changes to Meet the Goals.

    One option available to the safety professional is to modify current practices to bring the safety performance in line with the goals and standards. This may require the implementation of new programs, the modification or enforcement of current programs, or the selection of more appropriate performance measures that are indicative of the true levels of safety performance.

11. New or Modified Goals:

    Depending upon the results, the safety manager may have to reevaluate the safety performance goals to ensure they meet the organization's needs. Changes in production and job tasks may necessitate a change in the performance goals. With continual improvement as an underlying goal of safety performance, once a level of safety performance is met, improvement in the desired performance standards may be another reason for reevaluating the performance goals and standards.

Uses for Safety Performance Measurements

Safety performance measurements can have a variety of uses in the workplace. Some of the more common uses include control, self-assessment, continuous improvement, and management assessment (Training Resources and Data Exchange (TRADE) 1995, 1-7):

1. Safety Performance Control: Performance measure can be used to control losses, accidents, and injuries. By monitoring the extent to which these events are impacting an organization, corrective action can be identified and implemented to control accidents.

2. Self-Assessment of Safety Performance: Through the use of performance measurements and benchmarks, organizations can determine how good their safety performance is.

3. Continuous Improvement: As has been discussed previously, organizations can use safety performance measures to continually improve performance.

4. Management Assessment: Finally, safety performance measures can be used to assess management performance. These measures can be used to determine if the organization's objectives are being met, if the management structure and support is sufficient to implement the programs necessary to meet the safety performance goals, etc.

Outcome Measures

Quantitative safety performance measurements can be either outcome oriented or process oriented (Daugherty 1999, 147). Outcome-oriented performance measures are after-the-fact measures. The performance activity has occurred; then the results have been measured. Examples of outcome measures used in safety include the reduction in the number of accidents, lost workdays, etc. Outcome measures can provide an indication as to the impact safety program interventions have upon safety performance. These performance measures provide an historical account of the effectiveness of past performance.

One broad class of outcome measures commonly used to measure safety performance is called failure measures. These measures are generated from the injury recordkeeping system. Included in this group can be performance measured by "dollar" criteria. Losses and cost savings attributed to safety performance will often mean more to management than other safety measures such as frequency and severity rates.

Process-oriented performance measures are those measures indicative of action or activities performed. Process measures do not necessarily predict a program's outcome, though a carefully selected set of process variables can yield a valuable forecast of program outcomes (Daugherty 1999, 147). These measures indicate the extent to which an activity or process has been implemented. Safety process related measures include counting the number of safety training programs conducted, counting the number of safety inspections conducted, etc. Outcome measures can provide an indication as to the program's efficiency. Efficiency of a safety program is how well, how promptly, or how completely a program has been conducted in pursuit of the desired outcomes (Daugherty 1999, 147).

Performance Measures

Performance measurements are grouped into two categories: qualitative and quantitative. Qualitative safety measurements include checklists and narrative evaluations from accident report forms. Quantitative performance measures include any performance measures to which a number can be assigned. Measurement is crucial to achieving excellence in safety from two broad standpoints (Petersen 1998):

1. A macro-view—how overall results are measured to determine whether safety efforts are paying off. An example of a macro-view standpoint could include the accident trends experienced by a company over the previous year.
2. A micro-view—do measures ensure individual performance or foster nonperformance? From a micro-view standpoint, performance measures should be indicative of an individual's performance—i.e., how well a person is performing.

When selecting micro-view and macro-view measures, the performance measure should reflect an organizational process. Linking the safety measures to the organizational process provides a method for determining if the performance measures help the organization meet its goals and objectives.

In selecting measuring devices, a firm should use only activity measures at the lower managerial or unit levels, primarily activity measures (with some results measures) at the middle-upper management levels, and pure results measures for the executive level (Peterson, p. 40). The safety performance measures should be geared toward the employee's responsibilities and objectives. Employees at the supervisory and middle management level are focused on motivating employees to perform. Safety performance measures for employees at this level of the organization should aim toward motivating and directing employees to work in a safe manner.

At the middle and upper management level, outcome measures are the focus (Peterson 1998, 40). Managers at this level serve the primary function of providing supervision to ensure that the quality of work is being attained. Outcome-based safety performance measures for employees at this level can include results from inspections, job observations, and accident trends. Upper and middle managers use these performance measures to guide supervisors' activities so that the organization's safety goals are met. Since failure measures can be used a bit more at this level, traditional safety indicators become more useful (Peterson 1998, 40).

Categories of Performance Measures

Three broad classes of these measures are trailing indicators, current indicators and leading indicators. A good combination of trailing, current and leading indicators, based on the company's own needs, is always best (Dupont Corporation 2001).

Trailing Indicators

Trailing indicators are the traditional metrics that measure past safety efforts (Dupont Corporation 2000). When using trailing indicators, data is collected after the fact (after a number of accidents or illnesses, after two years of workers' compensation, etc.). Trailing indicators provide an organization with feedback in terms of how good performance has been over a period of time. Examples of trailing indicators include accident records, loss reports, injury and illness statistics, injury costs, and workers' compensation costs.

Some of the pros for using trailing indicators include the availability of the data and the ease with which the data can be compiled and presented. However, the safety professional must be able to draw some correlations between trailing initiators and actual safety program components and results. To be effective, a cause and effect relationship must be identified between the trailing indicators and the program procedures. The safety program procedures must be related to that which is being measured by the trailing indicators.

Current Indicators

Current indicators tell an organization how well the management systems are working now, as opposed to in the past (Dupont Corporation 2000). In addition, they provide a measure of potential losses over the short term. Examples of current indicators include measures of safe and unsafe acts, incident investigation reports and safety audits. Current indicators can provide the safety manager with immediate feedback on areas that require improvement.

Leading Indicators

Leading indicators are those measures that can be effective in predicting future safety performance (Dupont Corporation 2000). Leading indicators can be considered "before-the-fact" measures. These measures assess outcome actions taken before accidents occur and are measures of proactive efforts designed to minimize losses and prevent accidents. Leading indicators can help uncover weaknesses in the organization's operations or employee behaviors before they develop into full-fledged problems.

Examples of leading indicators include measures of the quality of an audit program, including schedule adherence, the number of repeat injuries, and analysis of process hazard reviews. As with trailing indicators, there must be some type of cause and effect relationship established between leading indicators and safety performance.

Safety sampling is a technique for measuring the effectiveness of safety before an accident occurs and thus can be used with leading indicators. Safety sampling involves taking periodic readings of how safely employees work and is based on the quality control principle of random sampling inspection, which is widely used to determine quality of production output without conducting complete inspections (Petersen 1998, 40).

Random sampling strategies can provide feedback as to the current condition of a safety program. Random sampling of employees performing job tasks and random sampling of the current status of workplace conditions are most often performed using audit and survey techniques. When conducted at random intervals, assumptions about the overall status of the safety program can be inferred from the audit results. In addition to the random selection, the safety manager that utilizes sampling strategies should also ensure that a sufficient sample size is obtained. As a general rule, the larger the sample size, the more likely the results obtained reflect the status of the entire population.

Implementing a Safety Performance System

Implementing a safety performance system starts with defining the job-performance objectives for the position to be analyzed. This will require a thorough and accurate analysis of the job. The most common task analysis method for analyzing jobs requires a decomposition of job tasks into simpler subtasks, component tasks, or steps (Kaufman, Thiagarajan, and Sivasailam 1997, 189). The safety field is familiar with this process, as it is a common approach to conducting safety-related analyses such as job safety analyses or procedure analyses. Selection of the job tasks to analyze should take into account past accident history, potential for catastrophic accidents, and the degree to which workers are exposed to potential hazards. When properly conducted, the observation of the job tasks should result in written, precise, and measurable job-performance objectives.

In addition to job tasks, the organizational processes must be evaluated and documented.

Benefits of Safety Performance Measurements

Safety performance measures have certain distinct advantages (Petersen 1998, 39).

- These measures are flexible and allow for individual supervisory styles. The same measure need not be used for all supervisors. They are excellent for use in objective-setting approaches.
- Feedback is swift, since most of these techniques require supervisors to report their level of performance to upper management. (They are also often self-monitoring.)
- They measure the presence, rather than the absence, of safety.
- They are usually simple and, thus, administratively feasible.

Additional benefits from performance measures include (Training Resources and Data Exchange (TRADE) 1995, 1-7):

- Providing an understanding of the management process
- Providing a factual basis for decision making in the organization
- Identifying areas for improvement
- Determining if improvements have occurred
- Identifying unforeseen problem areas

Shortcomings of Measurements

While the benefits of establishing and using measurements are numerous, there are also some shortcomings that can be experienced if the measurements are not properly defined and used. Examples of these shortcomings can include:

1. A cause and effect relationship between the measurement and the activity does not exist.
2. There are delays between the activity and the measurement.
3. Reliability in the measurement process may be lacking.
4. Outside factors may be influencing results, thus affecting the validity of the measurement.

Safety Objectives and Goals

Performance measures can be broadly classified as safety goals and safety objectives. Goals are more long range than objectives and they may or may not be quantitatively measurable, while objectives cover a shorter term and are always measurable (Pierce 1995, 125). Most often, objectives are goals that have been broken into small, progressive pieces. Six guidelines for setting goals and objectives are (Pierce 1995, 127):

1. Set goals and objectives as part of the planning process.
2. Word the goals and objectives clearly.
3. Goals and objectives must be realistic.
4. Accomplishing goals and objectives must be under the responsible person's influence or control.
5. Objectives must be assigned to someone.
6. Completion dates must be established for each objective and goal.

Establishing Safety Objectives

In order to develop an effective safety metrics program, the objectives of the organization must be clearly established. Business objectives typically state and define underlying organizational "values" and quality factors such as safety, rework, environmental soundness, and customer satisfaction. The development of these business objectives usually begins with the stated mission for the organization. This organization's mission statement will provide the overall guidance for not only the safety program but also any other program developed to meet the organization's overall goals and objectives.

While the business side of the objectives may be stated in terms of productivity, costs, or profits, safety objectives can be stated in terms of losses, accidents, safe behaviors, or increased costs.

Establishing Effective Goals

Establishing goals for the safety metrics program provides a vital blueprint for implementing and directing the organization's resources in order to achieve desired outcomes. The most commonly found goals in any safety and health program include lost-time injury rate, lost workdays, recordable injury rate, and total injury rates. Safety goals can also be vague. Some examples that fall into this category include goals "to achieve compliance" or "to provide a safe environment" (Pierce 1995, 122).

When establishing goals it is important to identify those measures that are indicative of a good program. They must emphasize activities that are needed to meet the goals.

A common downfall is to develop broad-ranging goals with no clear understanding of the activities that impact the outcomes, which in turn determine whether or not the goals are met. The best results for a metrics program can be achieved when the goals set are appropriate.

Guidelines for developing effective goals and objectives have been presented in this chapter. The following are some examples of poorly constructed and well-constructed safety goals and objectives:

- Poorly constructed safety goal: "Improve the safety record of the organization."

This is considered a poorly written safety goal since it does not establish a timeframe for completion. It also does not provide a specific outcome that would be indicative of meeting the goal.

- Well-constructed safety goal: "Over the next five years, the organization will reduce OSHA recordable injuries by 10 percent."

This is considered a well-constructed safety goal because it establishes a fixed long-term focus for the safety program. The desired outcome for the goal is also measurable.

- Poorly constructed safety objective: "The organization will increase employee safety training offerings."

This is considered a poorly written safety objective since it does not establish a timeframe for completion. It also does not provide a measure by which success or failure of meeting the objective can be ascertained.

- Well-constructed safety objective: "During this fiscal year, the organization will provide 12 monthly safety-training programs at which 90 percent of the employees shall attend."

This is considered a well-constructed safety objective because it establishes a fixed short-term focus for the safety program. The desired outcome for the goal is measurable.

Summary

Safety performance measurement is the process of establishing standards of performance and then measuring current safety performance against these standards. Safety performance begins with well-established goals and objectives and ends with corrective action that brings performance in line with the goals. Safety managers use performance measures to gauge progress towards these goals, answer key questions about the status of safety program activities, and identify areas that can be improved. A variety of performance measures—including leading, trailing, and current indicators—are available to the safety manager. A good performance measure program uses a combination of these different types.

Chapter Questions

1. Define performance measures.
2. What importance do performance measures have for an organization with regard to safety?
3. What type of process should one follow when developing performance measures?
4. Describe a methodology for implementing performance measures in the workplace.
5. Define key objectives, outcome measures, and activity measures.
6. Differentiate between qualitative measures and quantitative measures.
7. Describe three benefits of performance measures.

3

Statistical Methods in Safety Metrics

Proper safety metrics requires the proper analysis of the collected data. The purpose of the data analysis is to make comparisons between the results and the goals or benchmarks. Significant trends or differences between the obtained results and the benchmarks should be identified. There are a number of statistical procedures that can be used to determine if there are any trends in the data or if the results meet what is anticipated.

Using statistical techniques, one can establish the criteria to determine if trends and changes are occurring. Examples of criteria to apply to make this determination include continual improvement, "zero defects," cost-benefit analysis, and comparison against benchmark. There are also a number of statistical procedures available to the safety professional to identify relationships between safety program activities and measured outcomes. (One such technique is called a correlation procedure.) One must keep in mind however, that significant relationships between activities and safety performance measures do not necessarily indicate a cause and effect relationship. To illustrate this point, suppose a safety manager conducts training on proper lifting techniques to a group of employees. After a period of time, job observations indicate that the employees are practicing proper lifting, and records indicate that frequency of back injuries has decreased. A significant relationship is identified between the number of proper lifting observations and the number of back injuries using a correlation procedure.

Because a statistically significant relationship has been identified, the safety manager must determine why there are now fewer back injuries. To be able to state that the training activity caused the decrease in back injuries, a comparison must also be made to a group of workers that did not attend the training and the frequency of their back injuries. (This group is called the *control group*.) If statistical findings indicate that the group that attended the training had significantly fewer back injuries than those employees that did not attend, then a conclusion could be drawn that it was the training that caused the decrease in injuries. This control group is necessary to eliminate the possibility that another factor (such as back braces handed out to *all* employees at the time of the training) is not the cause of the decrease in injuries.

With an understanding as to why the results were obtained, follow-up action may be necessary. If it is determined that the results are stable (in other words, that the number of back injuries per week are not increasing or decreasing) and that performance changes are necessary (back injuries still occur too frequently), then it should be the process that is changed. If, however, the correlation between training program attendance and reported injuries is not significant, indicating no relationship between injury prevention and training (in other words, the training had no effect on the number of injuries per week), then follow-up activities should be conducted. The activities may include evaluating the training program to improve effectiveness or developing lifting procedures that can be used to achieve the desired results. Examples of strategies that can be used to evaluate activities include root cause analyses, re-engineering the process, developing changes to be made, and creating an implementation plan.

Prior to implementing the corrective action, an analysis of the safety metric used to determine success should also be conducted. Perhaps the frequency of back injuries is not a good measurement. It may not accurately indicate of the success of the training program. There could be many reasons for this. For example, suppose that following the training program, the number of employees engaged in lifting tasks increased dramatically, thus increasing the organization's exposure to back injuries. In this case, back injury "rates" (that is, the number of back injuries per person per week) may have decreased significantly, yet the total number of back injuries per week may have increased. Thus, the performance measure of frequency of back injuries is not a suitable measure of performance. The same analysis can then be applied to the frequency of back injuries per person and find that it is a suitable measure.

With the proper data to be collected identified, an assessment should be made to predict the anticipated improvement in the safety performance. Does one expect a decrease in back injury rates of 10 percent over the next year? Is a 20 percent decrease reasonable? Using past performance indicators (for example, successful training sessions decreased injuries 10 percent in past years) and professional judgment, the desired benefits can be used to define the performance goal. The last step is to implement the follow-up activity (change the process, alter the training, etc.) and conduct an assessment to determine the actual impact of the process change in the performance measure. In our example, a decision could be made to put all employees through the training session two times per year. After one year, the frequency of back injuries per person (or other appropriate performance measure) can be measured and compared with the performance goal.

Data Formats

Data can be classified into four major categories based upon the characteristics of the numbers. It is important for the safety manager to understand these categories because some kinds of data are more useful than others are. From least useful to most useful, the categories are: *categorical, ordinal, interval,* and *ratio* (Horvath 1974, 16).

Ratio data is the most useful because it can be used with all statistical procedures. Categorical data, on the other hand, is the least useful because it can only be used with statistical procedures designed specifically for categorical variables.

It is crucial to identify the format of the data because the various statistical methods that the data can be used with are dependent upon it. Researchers often use computers to analyze the data. Although a computer will provide an answer for a statistical test, it may be meaningless if the data format has violated the assumptions of the statistical procedure. For example, suppose a safety manager collects data on the gender of the employees injured over the past year. To input the data into the computer, she assigns a "1" to the females and a "2" to the males. If the safety manager attempts to find the mean (on average, what is the sex of the person injured?), the number the computer may return may be 1.5. This number is meaningless since it is does not correspond to a category (male or female).

Categorical Data

Categorical or *discrete data* represents categories. Examples of data that can be considered categorical are items that a person taking a survey can check in a box. Examples of categorical data include the gender of a person, the department that a person works in, and the classifications for occupational illnesses. Categorical data that can be classified into two groups is referred to as *dichotomous data,* as is the case for the gender of a person.

To establish categorical data, the researcher first must define the categories, ensuring that there are distinct differences between the possible groups and that a response cannot fall into more than one group. The values assigned to categorical data only serve to differentiate between memberships in the groups. Magnitude does not exist between category values. For example, it would not be correct to say that a category numbered "2" is twice as large as a category numbered "1." When collecting data for analysis, the researcher has two options for developing categories. The researcher may either define the categories and ask the respondent to select one or pose a question, collect the answers, and develop the categories from the responses.

Ordinal Data

Ordinal data is rank order data. Ordinal means that the data is ordered in some fashion. For example, rankings from best to worst, highest to lowest, or "poor, fair, good," etc., would be considered ordinal data. A safety manager could use this type of data to evaluate safety practices. For example, a survey that asked employees, "How often do you use protective gloves when handling chemicals?" and offered "almost always, often, seldom, and almost never" as choices would be an example of ordinal data.

Common examples of ordinal data are *Likert scales*. When a person is asked to select a number on a Likert scale (for example, evaluate the safety program from 1 to 5), it is possible to arrange the answers into some order from best to worst, highest to lowest, etc. An example of a Likert Scale is in Figure 3.1.

Strongly Disagree	Disagree	Undecided	Agree	Strongly Agree
1	2	3	4	5

Figure 3.1. Sample Likert Scale

One important aspect of ordinal data is that one cannot make comparisons between the values. For example, Respondent A assigned a ranking of a 4 to the scale item in Figure 3.1. Respondent B assigned a ranking of 2 to the same item. This does not indicate that Respondent A agrees twice as much as Respondent B. One can say however, that Respondent A is more agreeable to the item than Respondent B. In the other example above, it would be accurate to say that employees that indicated they "often" wear gloves, wear gloves more frequently than those that chose "seldom." However, it is not possible to give any values to these measurements. One cannot claim, for instance, that they wear gloves 60 percent of the time.

Interval Data

Interval data is a form of continuous data. *Continuous* means that all points along the line of data are possible (including fractional values). Interval data also has zero as a placeholder on the scale. An example of a scale that is interval is the Fahrenheit thermometer. Examples of interval data that a safety professional may use include temperature readings, job analysis scales, and environmental monitoring readings.

An interval scale is divided into equal measurements. In other words, the difference between 20 and 10 degrees Fahrenheit is the same as between 30 and 20 degrees Fahrenheit. However, it is not accurate to say that 20 degrees is twice as hot as 10 degrees Fahrenheit. When ratio comparisons like this cannot be made, the scale is said to not have "magnitude." Magnitude is an ability to make comparisons between the values of a scale.

Ratio Data

Ratio data is continuous data that does not have zero as an arbitrary placeholder. The zero on this scale represents an actual absence of that characteristic. For example, zero accidents recorded for a period of time means no accident cases existed. Ratio data is the only scale in which magnitude between values on the scale exists. If one group had 10 accidents and the other five, then it is correct to say that the first group had twice as many accidents as the second. Examples of ratio data that the safety professional would use include any characteristics that are counted, such as the number of accidents, the number of days away from work, etc.

Recoding

Recoding data is the process of sorting and assigning cases to newly defined variables. When analyzing data, the safety manager may need to recode data into different formats to increase the variety of statistical procedures that can be used and, as a result, increase the potential for identifying significant findings with the data. For example, a safety manager collects data pertaining to the age of the workers involved in an accident. The data is collected by asking the workers to write their age at the time of survey on a line. This data as we discussed earlier is considered ratio in format. The safety manager decides to break the respondents into groups according to age. A new variable is created called "age group" and the categories defined. Using the age value provided in the ratio format survey question, each respondent is now assigned a category value in the new age category variable. The new categorical variable can be used in the data analysis.

Strength of the Data Formats

As the format of your data moves from categorical to ordinal, to interval, and finally to ratio, the number of statistical tests you can use on the data increases. Categorical data provides the least flexibility in terms of statistical testing. It cannot be recoded. Ordinal data can be recoded into a categorical format but cannot be recoded into interval or ratio formats. Interval data can be recoded into ordinal and categorical formats. Ratio can be recoded into any of the data formats. As you can see, ratio data provides the greatest flexibility for statistical analysis. It can be used with any number of statistical procedures because the researcher can recode the data into any of the other data formats. For example, suppose the number of lost days for each accident is collected. This data is in ratio format. It can then be recoded into interval format by placing the number of days lost in order from least to greatest; this is an ordinal format. The number of lost days could also be assigned to categories such as 0–5 lost days, 6–10 lost days and so on, which would represent categorical data. The data can be represented by these three different formats, and as a result, statistical procedures for ratio, ordinal, and categorical data can be used. As a general rule, the more flexible the data format, the more options the researcher has available for analysis.

Descriptive Statistics

Descriptive statistics are techniques used to describe a population or sample. One cannot draw conclusions using descriptive statistics. For example, suppose a safety manager collects information from accident report forms about the age of workers that suffered a back injury. The average age for the sample was found to be 45 years old. The only conclusion the safety manager can make is that the average age of those persons from which the sample was selected is 45 years old. He or she cannot conclude that the average age for all people ever suffering from a back injury is 45 years of age, nor that the average age of those injured at another facility is 45 years old. He or she can only describe those injured in his or her sample at that time and location.

Commonly used descriptive statistics include measures that describe where the middle of the data is. These measures are sometimes called "measures of central tendency" and include the *mean, median,* and *mode.* Another category of measures describes how spread out the data is. These measures are sometimes called "measures of variability" and include the *range, variance,* and *standard deviation.* Additional descriptive measures can include percentages, percentiles, and frequencies. In safety performance measurement, the safety professional must determine the format of the data (i.e., ratio, interval, ordinal, or categorical) that will be collected and match the data format to the appropriate statistic. As will be discussed in the following sections, certain descriptive statistics are appropriate for certain data formats.

Measures of Central Tendency

The first group of descriptive statistics are the measures of central tendency. These statistics describe where the middle of the data falls. There are three measures of central tendency. They are the mean, median, and mode (Hays 1998, 155–56).

Mean

The *mean* is the arithmetic average of a group of numbers. The *arithmetic average* is found by adding up the items and dividing this sum by the number of items in the group. For example, a safety manager identified the number of lost workdays for five injury cases. The lost workdays were 5, 8, 15, 2, and 7. The average is calculated using the following formula:

mean = sum of the lost workdays / number of injury cases

Or in statistical notation:

$$\overline{X} = \frac{\Sigma x}{N}$$

Where:
$\overline{X}$ is the mean
Σx is the sum of the individual observations
N is the total number of observations

Mathematically, the following is performed:

$$\overline{X} = \frac{5+8+15+2+7}{5} = 7.4$$

Median

The median is the point that 50 percent of the values lie above and 50 percent lie below. Using the numbers of lost workdays from the example above, the median would be determined by first arranging the observations in order from lowest to highest. Thus, the observations would be arranged as 2, 5, 7, 8, and 15. Because there is an odd number of observations in this example, the median would be the number in the middle of the distribution. The median would be 7 in this example.

In situations where there is an even number of observations, the median is calculated by averaging the values of the middle two observations. For example, suppose a safety manager collected data from carbon monoxide sensors in the workplace. The carbon monoxide readings were 10 ppm, 15, ppm, 8, ppm, and 15 ppm. To calculate the median for an even number of observations, the data is arranged in order from lowest to highest and the average of the two middle readings is calculated. For this example, the data is arranged as 8 ppm, 10 ppm, 15 ppm, and 15 ppm. The center two readings are 10 ppm and 15 ppm. Taking the average of these two observations $[(10 + 15)/2]$, the median for this distribution is found to be 12.5 ppm.

Mode

The mode of a distribution is the most frequently occurring number in that distribution. Using the carbon monoxide data in case above, the value 15 ppm occurs twice while all other values appear only once in the distribution. In this example, the mode of the distribution is 15 ppm.

It is possible for a distribution to have more than one mode. In the distribution of numbers 2, 3, 4, 5, 5, 6, 7, 8, 8, 10, there are two modes, 5 and 8, since these values occur more frequently than the others do. This would be considered a bimodal distribution (2 modes).

Measures of Variability

There are three measures of variability. These measures indicate the spread of the data and are the range, variance, and standard deviation (Hays 1998, 171–76). Measures of variability provide the safety manager with an indication of how much the obtained results are spread out. For example, suppose a safety manager collects information on the number of lost days for three employees. The days lost are 1, 1, and 2 (that is, they range from 1 to 2 days). The measures of variability would be small compared to three employees who lost 1, 10, and 50 days (a range spread from 1 to 50 days). For various statistical procedures, the degree of variation in the data can impact the decision as to whether the results are significant or not.

Range

The range for a set of data is the difference between the lowest value and the highest value in the distribution. For example, suppose a safety manager collected data on the number of accidents reported by the various departments in a company for a given month. The number of accidents reported were as follows:

$$3, 2, 4, 5, 6, 8$$

Rearranging the distribution from lowest to highest, (2, 3, 4, 5, 6, 8), the range is calculated by subtracting the lowest value, 2, from the highest value, 8. The range is therefore $8 - 2 = 6$.

Variance

The variance of a distribution is a measure of how much the individual data points vary from the distribution mean, i.e., how "spread out" the data is. The variance is the average of the squared deviations from the mean and is calculated using the formula presented below. Using the data for the number of hazards identified in various locations above, the variance provides an indication as to how much the number of accidents reported differs from the average. (When the variance is calculated for a sample, as is the case in this example, the sum of the squared deviation scores is divided by $N - 1$, where N is the number of observations. When the variance is calculated for an entire population, the sum of the squared deviation scores is divided by N.)

Variance Formula

$$\sigma^2 = \frac{\sum (x - \bar{x})^2}{N - 1}$$

Where:

σ^2 is the variance
$\sum (x - x)^2$ is the sum of the deviation scores, squared
N   is the total number of observations

To calculate the variance using the data set above, the first step is to determine the average. Using the formula presented previously, we calculate the sample average using the following formula:

$$\bar{X} = \frac{\sum x}{N}$$

The average is calculated by adding the values for the individual observations and dividing by the number of observations.

$$\overline{X} = \frac{3+2+4+5+6+8}{6} = \frac{28}{6} = 4.7$$

Using the mean of 4.7, the difference between each data point and the average is calculated (Column 3). Table 3.1 depicts this process.

Table 3.1. Variance Example

Column 1	Column 2	Column 3	Column 4
Number of hazards identified	Mean	Difference between the number of hazards and the mean (Column 1 – Column 2)	Square of the differences (Column 3 ^{2})
3	4.7	−1.7	2.89
2	4.7	−2.7	7.29
4	4.7	−.7	.49
5	4.7	.3	.09
6	4.7	1.3	1.69
8	4.7	3.3	10.89
Total			23.34

The top summation term, $\sum (x - x)^2$ in the variance formula requires the statistician to sum the squared difference values for all cases. In this example, that total is 23.34 (see Table 3.1). The final step is to divide this sum by N − 1, where N represents the total number of cases. In this example, there are six cases so N = 6. The variance for this distribution is 4.67. The obtained value summarizes how different the case values are from each other. The value 4.67 provides meaning when comparisons are made to other variances.

Variance Calculation

$$\sigma^2 = \frac{23.34}{6-1} = 4.67$$

Standard Deviation

The average difference between the mean and a value is called the standard deviation. For example, in the case above, the difference between each measurement (the number of accidents reported) and the mean (4.7) is the standard deviation. The standard deviation is calculated by taking the square root of the variance.

$$\sigma = \sqrt{\sigma^2}$$

Where:

  σ is the standard deviation for the sample
  σ^2 is the variance for the sample

Using the accident data from above, the standard deviation would be calculated as follows:

$$\sigma = \sqrt{4.67} = 2.16$$

Therefore, on average, the number of reported accidents at any of the six sites will be 2.16 away from 4.7. Or, the number of accidents reported at each site, on average, will be 4.7 give or take 2.16. This is sometimes written as 4.7 ± 2.16.

The standard deviation can also be used to determine the expected ranges for scores in a given distribution. By definition, we expect to find approximately 68 percent of the population between +1 and −1 standard deviations, approximately 95 percent of the population between +2 and −2 standard deviations, and 99 percent of the population between +3 and −3 standard deviations. A population is the total number of possible sources from which data could be obtained. For example, all of the employees in a company could be defined as the population while those from which data is actually collected is called a sample. A sample is a subset of the total population.

The Normal Distribution

The *normal distribution* is expected when completely random, continuous data is collected from a population. The normal distribution is commonly referred to as the "bell-shaped" curve because of its shape, which resembles the outline of a bell. It is important for safety managers to become familiar with the normal distribution because the data they collect will most often be compared with this distribution. This comparison then may lead to conclusions about the population.

The normal distribution has three main properties (Kuzma 1992, 81). First, it has the appearance of a bell-shaped curve that extends infinitely in both directions. Second, it is symmetrical about the mean. Finally, the number of cases expected to be found between points follows a few specific percentages. For example, the entire curve represents 100% of the population. One would expect to find approximately 34% of the subjects in a population to obtain a score between the mean and one standard deviation. One would expect to find approximately 47% of the subjects in a population to obtain scores between the mean and two standard deviations. Between the mean and 3 standard deviations, one would expect to find 49.9% of the subjects. The normal distribution, or bell shaped curve, is presented in Figure 3.2.

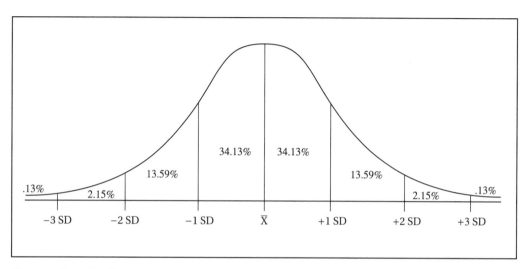

Figure 3.2. Bell Shaped Curve

Probability

Probability is the likelihood that an event will occur (Witte and Witte 1997, 190). Probability is a useful concept for safety managers because it helps them distinguish between results that are caused by their safety efforts and results that are due to random fluctuations in the data. For example, for the last two months, accidents in a chemical plant have averaged 3 incidents per month, down from a yearly average of 4 per month. Is this due to the new safety initiative? Or does the data merely indicate the normal ups and downs of any measurement over time? A safety manager can determine this through examining the probability that the change in the data is due to random chance. If the likelihood of obtaining this result totally due to chance is remote, the statistician may conclude that the results are "statistically significant"— in other words, that the data reflects a real change in the safety of the plant.

It is important for the safety manager to note that probability and possibility are two different concepts. Possibility determines whether or not an event *can* occur; probability is the likelihood or chance that it *will*. One can determine probabilities for events or occurrences and one can determine probabilities for analysis outcomes. To determine probabilities of events, the safety manager determines the likelihood that it will occur.

Probabilities are determined for events. An event can be an occurrence of any type—for example, an accident, incident, near miss, etc. The letter "P" is used to signify probability and the letters A, B, C, etc., are used to identify different events. Using this system, P(A) represents the probability of event "A." The term P(B) represents the probability of event "B" (which is a different event than "A"). Probability values are derived as decimal values, then converted to a percentage and read as such. An obtained probability value of .05 is equivalent to a 5% probability. For example, let the event "A" stand for a chemical spill; then the probability of a chemical spill this month is written as P(A). If the safety manager has calculated that P(A) = .12, this means that there is a 12% probability of a chemical spill this month.

Probability Rules

There are rules that apply to probabilities that allow safety managers to manipulate and interpret the results (Hays 1988, 22–25). For example, suppose a safety manager wanted to find the probability that there is *not* a chemical spill this month. Something "not happening" is not an event; however, the safety manager can use the following rules and concepts to determine this probability anyway.

1) The probability of an event must be between 0 and 1.00. A probability of zero means an event will not happen. A probability of 1 means an event is certain to happen. (This rule is called the *rule of probability range*.)

2) For every event A, there is also a *complementary event* $\overline{A}$, read as "not A."

3) The sum of the probabilities of events A and $\overline{A}$ is always 1.00. This is called the *rule of complementary probability.*

In the example above, if A is a spill, then its complementary event, $\overline{A}$, is "there is no spill." According to the rule of complementary probability, $P(A) + P(\overline{A}) = 1$. (This is simply another way of saying that there will either be a spill or there will not.) Therefore, if the safety manager wanted to find the probability of there not being a spill, he or she could calculate $P(A) = 1 - P(\overline{A})$. From above, P(A) = .12, therefore $P(\overline{A}) = 1 - .12 = .88$, or an 88% probability that there will not be a spill this month.

Simple Probabilities

In a *simple event* probability, the researcher compares the number of times an event occurred compared to the total number of possible outcomes.

Simple Event Formula

The formula for calculating simple event probabilities is as follows (Hays 1988, 27):

$$P(A) = \frac{\text{\# of wanted events}}{\text{total number of possible events}}$$

Simple Event Example

Suppose a safety manager collected data from accident reports involving back injuries. Over a three-year period, 300 reports were filed, of which 18 involved back injuries. Using the simple event formula, the probability of randomly selecting a report for which a back injury was recorded from the 300 reports filed is determined by:

P(A) = 18 / 300 = .06 or a 6% chance of selecting a report involving a back injury from the 300 filed.

Joint Event Probabilities

A *joint event* is an event in which the researcher asks the question "What is the probability of event A and event B occurring at the same time?" An example of this may be determining the probability of an accident involving a particular model of forklift and the operator has less than 5 years of experience. To determine this, the safety manager must multiply the probability of the independent events together. In this context, two events are said to be "independent" if the occurrence of one event has no impact on the occurrence of the other. In this example, the independent event probabilities would be the probability of an accident involving a particular model of forklift and the probability of having an operator that has less than 5 years of experience. The formula for determining joint probabilities, given two independent events, is as follows (Hays 1988, 37):

$$P(A \text{ and } B) = P(A) \times P(B)$$

Where:
    P(A and B) is the probability of Event A and Event B
    P(A)   is the probability of Event A
    P(B)   is the probability of Event B

Joint Event Example

In this example, a safety manger wishes to determine the probability of an employee being involved in a vehicle accident and the driver has fewer than five years of experience with the company. An analysis indicates that the probability of any one employee having fewer than five years of experience is .03 or a 3% chance. The probability of any one employee being involved in a motor vehicle accident in a given year is .01 or a 1% chance. To calculate the probability of an employee with fewer than five years of experience and being involved in an accident, the probabilities of the two independent events are multiplied together:

$$P(A \text{ and } B) = P(A) \times P(B) = (.03 \times .01) = .0003 \text{ or } .03\% \text{ chance of being involved in an accident and having fewer than five years of experience.}$$

Compound Probabilities

There may be situations in which the safety manager must determine the probability of the occurrence of more than one possible event. For example, instead of determining the probability of all events occurring at the same time, one may wish to determine the probability of one or more event at a time. These probabilities are referred to as *compound probabilities*. One example of a compound probability would be determining the probability that either component A or component B fails at any time. To take another example, suppose the safety manager wishes to determine the probability of the forklift being involved in an accident *or* an accident involving an operator with less than 5 years of experience. The overall probability of a compound event is determined by summing the individual event probabilities together, keeping in mind that the sum of all events must not exceed 1.00. The term "or" represents addition in compound probabilities.

The safety manager must also determine when two events are *mutually exclusive*—meaning that only one event can occur at one time. In other words, one event prevents the second event from happening. This becomes critical in compound event calculations.

Suppose a safety manager wishes to determine the probability of an accident involving a Smith Semi Truck or a driver that has less than five years of experience. Past accident records indicate that Smith Semi Trucks were involved in 20% of all motor vehicle accidents while drivers with less than 5 years of experience were involved in 5% of all motor vehicle accidents. Using the formula for a compound event, the statistician would add the probability of an accident involving a Smith Semi (20%) to the probability of a driver with less than 5 years of experience (5%). Adding the two probabilities together yields 25%. However, because these events are not mutually exclusive, a problem arises: the safety manager has counted the accidents that involve Smith Semis and drivers with less than 5 years of experience twice. If the events are not mutually exclusive, meaning both events can occur at the same time, then the statistician must subtract out the probability of both events occurring at the same time. The compound event formula provides for this correction. The correct probability for an accident involving a Smith Semi truck or a driver with less than 5 years of experience would be as follows:

P (Smith Semi) + P (Driver with < 5 years of experience)
− P (Smith Semi & Driver < 5 yrs of experience)

(.20) + (.05) − (.20 x .05) = .24 or 24%

The formula for a compound event is as follows (Horvath 1974):

$$P(A \text{ or } B) = P(A) + P(B) - P(A \times B)$$

Where:
  P(A or B) is the probability of Event A or Event B
  P(A)   is the probability of Event A
  P(B)   is the probability of Event B

Compound Event Example

Suppose a safety manager in a chemical manufacturing plant obtained records for the plant. In the past year, there were 250 fires. The primary cause of the fires was determined to be an accidental spill of a flammable chemical in 108 cases, spontaneous ignition of a stored flammable chemical in 95 cases, arson in 12 cases, and of unknown origin in 35 cases. The safety manager would like to know what is the probability of having a fire with a primary cause due to an accidental spill of a flammable chemical or arson. Because the manager is determining a probability of "one or the other," she will be determining a compound event. The manager must then determine whether the events are mutually exclusive or not. To do this she must answer the question "can one claim to have a primary cause of an accidental spill of a flammable chemical and a primary cause of arson?" The manager determined that this is not possible; therefore the events are mutually exclusive and the probability of both events occurring at the same time is zero.

P(spill or arson) = P(spill) + P(arson) − P(spill and arson)

P(spill or arson) = (108 / 250) + (12 / 250) − (0) = .48 or 48% chance of having a fire due to an accidental spill of a flammable chemical or arson as the primary cause. The consultant can then compare these fire probabilities to what is expected from past records to determine if there are significant differences. Such significant differences could indicate potential areas of concern.

Conditional Probabilities

In a *conditional probability,* some condition or restriction is placed upon the sample. (Witte and Witte 1997, 193–94). This results in a smaller, more specific subset of the sample from which the safety manager can calculate more accurate probabilities. Using the vehicle accident presented earlier, a conditional probability could be formulated as follows: given the fact that an accident occurred involving a Smith Semi, what is the probability that the driver had less than 5 years of experience? The population in this example is narrowed from all vehicle accidents down to only those accidents involving Smith Semis. Within this specific subset, the probability of a driver having less than 5 years of experience is determined.

In conditional probabilities, the symbol "|" is shorthand for the phrase "given the fact." A conditional probability of P(A|B) is read as "the probability of A, given the fact that B has occurred." The formula for calculating a conditional probability is (Witte and Witte 1997, 193–94):

$$P(A|B) = \frac{P(A \text{ and } B)}{P(B)}$$

Where:

P (A|B)   is the probability of Event A given the fact that Event B has occurred
P (A and B) is the probability of A x B
P (B)   is the probability of Event B

In the motor vehicle accident example, the probability of having a driver with less than 5 years of experience given the fact that a Smith Semi was involved in the accident is:

$$P(A|B) = \frac{.20 \times .05}{.20} = .05 \text{ or } 5\% \text{ chance}$$

Conditional Probability Example

The probability of being involved in an accident from a chemical spill at a chemical manufacturing plant was determined to be 30 out of 100 accidents reported or 30%. The probability of the accident resulting in lost workdays was determined to be 10 out of every 100 accidents reported or 10%. The safety manager wishes to determine the probability of an accident resulting in lost workdays given the fact the accident was due to a chemical spill. First, he or she calculates the probability of a chemical spill accident resulting in lost workdays:

let   P(A) = probability that the accident is a chemical spill

and let P(B) = probability that the accident results in lost workdays

Then,

P (A & B) = (30 / 100) × (10 / 100) = .03

The conditional probability of a lost workday case given the fact that a chemical spill accident was reported would then be calculated by:

P (A|B) = P (A & B) / P(B) = .03 / .10 = .30 or a 30% chance of the accident resulting in lost workdays given the fact it was a chemical spill accident.

Binomial Probabilities

In situations where there are only two possible outcomes for an event—such as a "male/female" or "yes/no" situation—the distribution is said to be *binomial*. Observing a safety valve a number of times and determining the probability that it will be open or closed a specific number of times meets the binomial probability since there are only two possible outcomes, open or closed. The formula presented below can be used to determine the binomial probability (Hays 1988):

$$P = \frac{n!}{r!(n-r)!}(p^r)(1-p)^{(n-r)}$$

Where:
  P is the probability of the binomial event
  n is the total number of observations
  r is the number of desired outcome events
  p is the probability of the desired event occurring one time
  ! is the factorial of the value

The factorial of a number is written as an exclamation point after the number and means to multiply by all preceding whole numbers. For example,

5! = 5 × 4 × 3 × 2 × 1 = 120.

Operations in parenthesis are always performed first. For example,

(5-1)! = 4! = 4 × 3 × 2 × 1 = 24.

Binomial Probability Example

A safety inspector observes a safety valve 5 times and finds that it is open 4 of the 5 times. Past observations have indicated that there is a 50% chance at any given time that the valve will be open. What is the probability the inspector's observation? That is, what is the probability of observing this valve 5 times and finding it open 4 times? In the binomial probability formula, n is equal to the number of observations—in this case, the number of times the valve is observed; so n = 5. The number of desired events (the valve is found in the open position) is r, so r = 4. And the probability of one event (in this case the probability of the valve being open), is p = .5. So entering these values into the binomial probability formula gives:

$$P = \frac{n!}{r!(n-r)!}(p^r)(1-p)^{(n-r)}$$

$$P = \frac{5!}{4!(5-4)!}(.5^4)(1-.5)^{(5-4)} = .16 \text{ or } 16\% \text{ chance of the valve being open 4 times}$$
$$\text{when making 5 observations}$$

P   is the probability of the binomial event
N = 5 (total number of observations)
r = 4 (number of times the valve is open)
p = .5 (the probability of the valve being open at any one observation)

Poisson Probability

Poisson probability is one of the most useful probabilities available to the safety professional. A *Poisson probability* is used to determine the probability of an event when the frequency of its occurrence is quite low compared to the overall exposure, as is the case with accidents. For example, a company may experience 2 recordable injuries in the workplace based on 300,000 hours of exposure. Few occurrences (2 accidents) and large exposures (300,000 hours) indicate a *Poisson distribution* of data.

The Poisson probability formula uses an *expected number of mishaps* based upon previous experience (Hays 1988, 144–45).

$$P(X) = \frac{e^{-M} M^X}{X!} \qquad M = (N)(p)$$

e = base of a natural logarithm or 2.178
N = exposure period
p = probability of one mishap
X = number of mishaps in question
M = Expected number of mishaps during an exposure period
!   is the factorial of the value (for example $3! = 3 \times 2 \times 1$, $4! = 4 \times 3 \times 2 \times 1$, etc.)

Poisson Probability Example

Suppose accident data revealed that 4 defective components were found in 30,000 units shipped to the marketplace. A product liability prevention program was established to reduce the number of defective units sent to the marketplace. After the program was implemented, 50,000 more units were shipped to marketplace from which 3 were identified as having defective components. What was the probability of having 3 defective units in the 50,000 shipped based upon prior history?

The first step is to find the expected number of failures, M. This is determined by multiplying the number of exposure units (N) by the probability of one failure (p). There were 50,000 units shipped, which represents the exposure. The probability of a defective unit is $4/30,000 = 1.33 \times 10^{-4}$ based upon the previous units shipped. With the 50,000 units, one would expect $50,000 \times 1.33 \times 10^{-4} = 6.7$ defective units.

The next step is to plug the values into the formula. In the Poisson probability equation, the term "e" is the base of a natural logarithm, which is approximately equal to 2.718, and the variable "X" represents the specific number of defective units being investigated. In this example, X=3. Therefore, we have:

$$P(X) = \frac{e^{-M} M^{X}}{X!} \qquad M = (N)(p)$$

Where:
  P (X) is the Poisson probability of having 3 defective units out of 50,000 units shipped
  e   is the base of a natural logarithm or 2.718
  M $= (N \times p)$ or $(50,000 \times 1.33 \times 10^{-4}) = 6.7$
  X   is the number of unwanted events. In this example 3 failures

$$P(3 \text{ failures in 50,000 units}) = \frac{2.718^{-6.7}\, 6.7^{3}}{3!} = .06 \text{ or } 6\% \text{ chance of 3 defective units in 50,000 units shipped}$$

If one uses the cutoff point of .05 or 5% random chance, then the result of a 6% chance of finding 3 defective units in 50,000 is not significant; therefore, the safety manager can conclude the product liability program has not significantly reduced the number of defective units being shipped.

Practical Applications for Descriptive Statistics and Probabilities

There are a many situations in which a safety professional may need to use various descriptive statistics for data collected in the workplace. The following examples illustrate the use of descriptive statistics such as the mean, standard deviation, normal distribution, and probability.

Fire Protection and Insurance Application of Descriptive Statistics

A very common use for descriptive statistics is when a safety manager is asked to present data at company or regional meetings on losses incurred. Suppose a safety manager was asked to present the fire losses experienced by the plant over the previous three years. The following data was collected for insurance claims involving fires:

1999		2000		2001	
Department	Severity	Department	Severity	Department	Severity
Production	$1,900	Production	$3,800	Production	$6,300
Production	$2,200	Production	$6,300	Production	$5,600
Production	$4,500	Shipping	$9,000	Shipping	$4,600
Shipping	$3,500	Shipping	$2,000	Packaging	$500
Packaging	$400	Packaging	$700		

Descriptive statistics for the data above can be used to describe the losses by year as follows:

Year (s)	N	Range	Mean	Standard deviation
1999	5	4100	2500	1570.0
2000	5	8300	4360	3338.1
2001	4	5800	4250	2595.5
Total (1999–2001)	14	8,600	3664	2560.2

Descriptive statistics for the data above can be used to describe the losses by department as follows:

Department	N	Range	Mean	Standard deviation
Production	7	4400	4371	1831.0
Shipping	4	7000	4775	3011.5
Packaging	3	300	533	152.8
Total	14	8,600	3664	2560.2

Results in these tables provide the safety manager with a method for describing the losses. For example, when examined by year, 2000 had the highest average losses with $4,360. By department, the shipping department had the highest average losses with $4,775. The production department may have a frequency problem with their accident involvement, which is indicated by the fact that 50% of the reported accidents were from this department.

Ergonomics Application of Means, Standard Deviations, and the Normal Distribution

A safety manager was asked to determine if an emergency shut-off switch was located at a height that workers could be expected to reach in the event of an emergency. The switch had been placed at 79 inches from the floor. Anthropometric tables provided the safety manager with average standing overhead reach for the population of 85.5 inches and a standard deviation of 3.3 inches. Using the normal distribution curve, the safety manager can determine the overhead reach at each standard deviation and compare it to the corresponding percentage of the population. At 2 standard deviations below the mean, he or she can conclude that the overhead reach height is approximately 79 inches [(85.5) + (−2×3.3)]. Therefore, approximately 98% of the population could be expected to have an overhead reach of at least 79 inches. If the emergency handle were placed at this height, approximately 2% of the population would not be able to reach it.

Systems Safety Application of Probabilities

Probability formulas can be used in a variety of situations in which the investigator wishes to determine 1) the chances that an event will occur in the future, or 2) if an event has occurred, what were the odds of it occurring. One must select the appropriate probability formula depending on the question posed. In this example, a system safety engineer wanted to determine the probability that a particular transistor component on a circuit board was the cause for a failure during operation. The circuit board had five identical transistor components numbered one through five. The systems safety manager answered the following probability questions:

When the board fails, what is the probability that the failure was due to transistor #1?

1/5=.20 or 20% probability that transistor #1 failed.

When the board fails, what is the probability that the failure was due to transistor #1 or #2?

1/5+ 1/5−(1/5×1/5)=.36 or 36% probability that transistor #1 or #2 failed.

When the board fails, what is the probability that the failure was due to transistor #1 and #2?

1/5×1/5=.04 or 4% probability that transistor #1 and #2 failed at the same time.

General Industrial Safety Application of the Binomial Probability

Safety managers can use binomial probabilities in a variety of situations to determine the probability of a particular outcome. In this application, a safety manager has collected safety inspection data over a period of time for a particular power press. A summary of the inspection data is as follows:

Date	Warning Light Working Properly	Comments
1/13/99	Y	
1/20/99	N	Light replaced
1/27/99	Y	
2/5/99	Y	
2/12/99	Y	
2/19/99	Y	
2/26/99	Y	Warning light wiring harness changed with cheaper model.
3/6/99	N	Light replaced
3/13/99	N	Light replaced
3/20/99	N	Light replaced
3/27/99	N	Light replaced
4/5/99	Y	

During the inspections that occurred during January to February, the safety manager found the light to be burnt out during approximately 14% of the inspections, which approximates the percentage from previous years. Following a change in the wiring harness, the safety manager found the light to be burnt out during 80% of the inspections. The safety manager assumes that he has a 14% chance of finding a burnt out light but sees that there were 4 burnt out lights in 5 inspections during March. The odds of finding this number of burnt out lights in 5 inspections can be determined using the Binomial Probability function.

$$P = \frac{5!}{4!\,(5-4)!}(.14^4)(1-.14)^{(5-4)}$$

$$P = .008$$

Based upon this result, the probability of having 4 burnt out lights during 5 inspections is .8%. This means that if the light is burning out just by chance, there is a .8% chance of obtaining these inspection results. Typically, when results occur at a probability of 5% or less, they are statistically significant. In other words, it is highly unlikely that the light is burning out by chance—the statistical evidence indicates that something is causing it to burn out. In this situation, one would suspect that the changed wiring harness may be contributing to the burnt out lights, assuming all other variables have remained the same. However, probabilities and correlations do not show cause and effect. Changing the wiring harness back to the original type, monitoring the frequency of burnt out lights, and establishing the fact that the frequency of burnt out lights has decreased is one method of showing cause and effect.

Summary

A critical step in the establishment and use of safety performance measures is the analysis of collected data. An understanding of the various data formats (categorical, ordinal, interval, and ratio) and statistical procedures will provide the safety manager with valid and reliable results. When correctly analyzed, activities designed to improve safety performance will have a greater impact upon performance and future measures. Descriptive measures allow the safety manager to describe the safety performance status in the workplace. These measures fall into two categories: those that describe the "center" of the data (mean, median, and mode) and those that describe how "spread out" the data is (range, variance, and standard deviation).

Statistical procedures, such as correlations, indicate relationships between two or more factors. Inferential statistics and probabilities allow the safety manager to reach conclusions about the safety performance measures (e.g, has the training had a real effect or is the reduction in accidents due to chance alone) and to have a degree of certainty about the findings.

Chapter Questions

1. Define the measures of central tendency and the measures of variability.
2. The following data was collected from CJD Industries over a 12 month period:

Month	Number of Injuries
January	5
February	8
March	9
April	5
May	4
June	6
July	7
August	4
September	8
October	9
November	5
December	4

   Calculate the mean, median, mode, standard deviation, range, and variance for the number of injuries that occurred per month.
3. Differentiate between ordinal, nominal, ratio, and interval data formats.
4. What percentage of the population would expect to fall between the mean and two standard deviations?
5. If it was determined that the probability of a system failure due to component A is .0003 and the probability of a system failure due to component B is .0001, what is the probability of a system failure due to A and B?
6. If it was determined that the probability of a system failure due to component A is .0002 and the probability of a system failure due to component B is .0004, what is the probability of a system failure due to A or B assuming A and B could occur at the same time?

7. It was determined that the probability of having one accident during a five-day workweek was .003. What is the probability of having exactly 3 accidents in a five-day work week?

8. What are the probability formulas for a joint event, compound event, and simple event probability?

9. What is the maximum value a probability can have?

10. Describe the impact data representing a sample versus a population has upon calculating a variance and standard deviation.

4

Run Charts and Control Charts

A *control chart* is a statistical device used for the study and control of safety performance in the workplace. The basis of control chart analysis is the knowledge of chance variations in the data (Duncan 1974, 375). If a series of safety measurements are plotted and the obtained measurements are truly random, the distribution would approximate the normal bell-shaped curve. Plotting the data on a control chart, one would obtain measurements over time that fall into the ranges depicted in Figure 4.1, with more measures occurring at or near the average more frequently and readings at the extreme ends of the possible measurements infrequently.

Control charts are used in safety to detect significant changes in performance measures and to ascertain whether the performance measures are within an acceptable range. The acceptable range for a control chart is established using control limits. When the data points fall outside of the control limits, a significant change has occurred and an investigation should be conducted. To reinforce this idea, it is useful to document the "owner" of each performance measure and the management decisions that have been, or will be made based upon this measure (Department of Energy, Hanford Site 2001).

Run Charts

A run chart is a preliminary display of safety performance indicator data (Department of Energy, Hanford Site 2001). The run chart is a graphic representation of the raw data over time without the presence of the average, upper control limits, and lower control limits. When using the data from a run chart to construct a control chart, it is important that the data obtained for the control chart is coming from the same type of sample that the run chart was constructed with. If the characteristics of the subjects from which the control chart data is being constructed from differ significantly from those that the run chart was constructed from, significant values may be obtained not because of actual significantly different performance, but rather because of differences in the subjects.

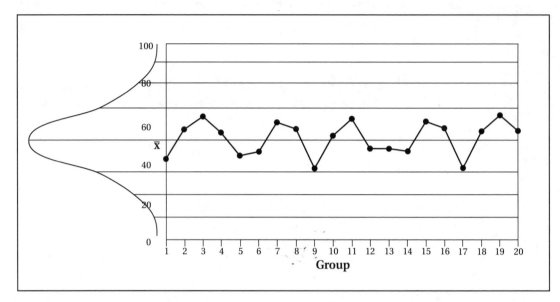

Figure 4.1. Theoretical Basis for the Control Chart

For example, suppose a safety manager collected data on back injuries over a period of time. At some point, a new back injury awareness program is started which includes a more aggressive reporting program. As one may expect, the number of reported back injuries increase, thus producing a run chart in which the data appears to indicate a worsening problem—a rise in the number of back injuries. However, the run chart data do not reflect a true decline in the safety of the facility, but rather the effects of implementing a new injury-reporting program. As a result of the lack of homogeneity in the data collected, the run chart does not truly indicate the injury experience over time. A better alternative is to use the data from the new reporting program as a baseline rather than analyze it in comparison to prior data.

Developing Run Charts

Developing a run chart begins with defining the items you want to track. If, for example, the run chart will be used to track injuries, a definition of what constitutes an injury should be established. This provides consistent data collection and helps validate the results of the run chart. The measurement tracked (such as injuries) is plotted on the y-axis.

Scaling of the y-axis should be from zero through the highest data value (or highest control limit value). Starting the y-axis at a value higher than zero is to be avoided, as most people expect graph scales to be zero-based and linear. When a value plotted on the graph appears to be twice as large as the previous value, most people assume that the data has doubled. Starting the scale at a non-zero value may skew this perspective, and should be avoided unless absolutely necessary to see trends in the data. Time is plotted on the x-axis, and the time intervals should be equally spaced.

The process for setting up a run chart is as follows (Department of Energy, Hanford Site 2001):

1. Define the item that one wishes to measure (e.g., injuries, accidents, etc.).
2. Collect a sufficient amount of homogeneous data to construct the run chart.
3. Establish the scale for the Y-axis and label.
4. Establish the scale for the X-axis and label.
5. Gather the data for each time interval.
6. Plot each datum point on the graph.
7. Connect the points with line segments.

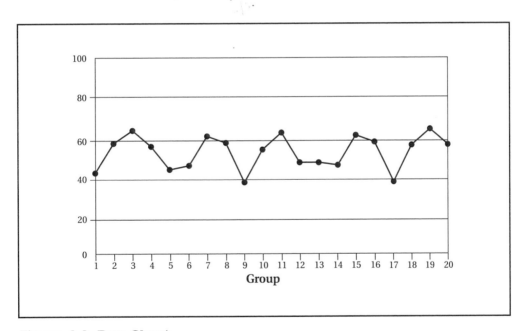

Figure 4.2. Run Chart

Run Tests

A *run up* is a succession of increases in value, and a *run down* is a succession of decreases (Duncan 1974, 386). The run refers to the increases or decreases, not to the numbers that produce the increases or decreases. For example, a series of measurements that were 2, 5, 8, 9, and 11 would be considered a run up of 4. A series of measurements that produced results of 18, 15, 12, 7, and 4 would be considered a run down of 4. Figure 4.3 represents a run up of 4.

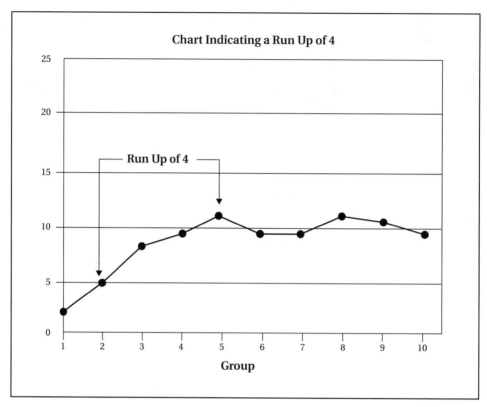

Figure 4.3. Data Run Up

Runs can be important in a number of ways when examining run charts and control charts. Two useful methods are (1) to count the total number of runs of any given class and (2) to note the length of the longest run of a given type (Duncan 1974, 387). The probabilities of the number of runs and the length of runs appearing at random in a run chart can also be estimated for the purpose of finding statistically significant plots of data. Suppose, for example, a safety manager in a water-bottling plant noted that a run chart of near accidents in the last year contained 7 runs up. If he or she also knew that run charts (of one year) with random data typically contain only 4 runs up, then the data may indicate an increase in the number of near accidents. The probability of a run chart with 7 runs up due only to chance could, in fact, be something very small, such as 4%. This would then be a good indication of statistically significant data.

Control Charts

A *control chart* is a run chart with the addition of a line indicating the mean and two lines indicating upper and lower control limits. A common *upper control limit* (UCL) is three standard deviations above the mean, and a common *lower control limit* (LCL) is three standard deviations below the mean. The calculation of control limits depends on the type of control chart. In general, if the data could not possibly be less than zero, e.g., a negative number of reports written, or a negative time period, then the LCL is assumed to equal zero.

In order to calculate control limits and the mean for variable charts, samples of size 4 or 5 observations are usually used; whereas for attribute charts, samples of 50 to 100 observations are most often used (Juran and Godfrey 1999, 45–47). For example, when constructing a variable control chart such as an X chart, samples of 4 to 5 observations are collected over a period of time with each sample collected over equal intervals. After 30 samples have been collected, the sample averages of 4 to 5 observations can be calculated, and then an overall average for the 30 sample averages. The overall average of the 30 samples is then used to construct the upper and lower control limits.

The more data points used to calculate the average and control limits, the more likely the data is representative of what is being measured, and the less likely fluctuations will result. It is also better to take small samples frequently than a single large sample. Experience is usually the best method for deciding on the frequency of taking samples (Juran and Godfrey 1999, 45–47). Further methods for calculating the upper and lower control limits for various types of control charts will be discussed in detail in the following sections.

Out-of-Control Criteria

The purpose of constructing the control chart is to graphically identify trends in data that indicate areas that must be addressed. When using control charts, safety managers will want to note data that is a "trend" or data that is "out of control." Data that consistently falls between the upper and lower control limits, or data that is "in control," may indicate that the control limits need to be recalculated with the more current data, thus tightening the control limits and thereby further improving the expected performance levels.

There are various criteria that have been established that define a control chart as being *"out of control."* These criteria are (Duncan 1974, 392):

1. One or more points outside the limits on a control chart.
2. One or more points in the vicinity of a warning limit. This suggests the need for immediately taking more data to check on the possibility of the process being out of control.
3. A run of 7 or more points. This might be a run up, a run down, or simply a run above or below the central line on the control chart.
4. Cycles or other patterns in the data. Such patterns may be of great help to the experienced operator.

Other criteria that are sometimes used are the following:

5. A run of 2 or 3 points outside of 2-sigma limits (2 standard deviations).

6. A run of 4 or 5 points outside of 1-sigma limits (2 standard deviations). When applying the out of control criteria, it is important to note that when using any statistical based procedure such as control charts and out of control criteria, the chances of finding an "out-of-control" chart increases as the number of out of control criteria applied to the chart increases. For example, one may be more likely to classify a chart as out of control when applying 5 criteria than when one applies only one criterion. This could be due not to the fact that there is a problem but rather due to the fact that so many criteria were applied. An out-of-control finding when the process is really not out of control is referred to as a false positive. To reduce the chances of false positives for control charts, one should evaluate the control chart using longer runs of data (Duncan 1974, 393).

Interpreting Control Charts

Control chart criteria such as the mean, upper control limit, and lower control limit are developed using data from past records. As current data points are collected, they are placed on the chart and monitored. Data that lie outside of the control limits, data that are trending in a direction (i.e., run ups or run downs), and data that are classified as "out of control" require special attention from the safety professional. Data runs (either up or down) indicate that something may be influencing the environment from which the data is being collected. For example, in a control chart that is monitoring recordable injury rates, a run up over successive periods indicates a worsening performance area. A run down for injury rates may indicate that safety interventions directed at reducing injury rates may be having an effect.

Data points consistently above the upper control limit indicate that the data is significantly different from what was expected. Points above the upper control limit could indicate problem if the data represents recordable injuries, or they may indicate a good thing if the data represents the number of positive safety contacts made between supervisors and employees. The same type of scenario holds true for points that are consistently below the lower control limit.

When points that represent a positive aspect consistently lie outside of the upper or lower control limits, one should consider reconstructing the control chart using the current data. By doing so, the safety manager can shift the mean, upper control limit, and lower control limit so that ranges on the control chart will more closely reflect the current data being collected. On the other hand, if points that represent a negative aspect consistently lie outside of the upper or lower control limits, it is imperative for the safety professional to evaluate the circumstances that are causing the results and implement the appropriate corrective measures.

If data on the control chart display wide fluctuations, with points both above and below the control limits, the chart is said to be "out of control." In this case, it is up to the safety manager to analyze the circumstances behind the data. Only through careful analysis can he or she identify the root cause of the fluctuations. Appropriate counter-measures should then be developed and implemented.

Treatment of Significant Changes

If any of the criteria for out of control data exist in constructing a new control chart, the average control limits may need to be calculated (Department of Energy, Hanford Site 2001). One may need to recalculate the control chart when it is determined that the process or activity being monitored had undergone a significant change, thus making the data being collected in the future significantly different that what would have been obtained had the process not undergone the change.

To illustrate an example of when it may be necessary to recalculate a control chart due to significant changes the following scenario was constructed:

A safety manager decided to construct a control chart to monitor the average num-ber of lost workdays per OSHA recordable case for the production department in a paper manufacturing company. The safety manager collected the data from the pre-vious three years' OSHA logs and calculated the average number of days per month along with the upper and lower control limits. Using the newly constructed control chart, the safety manager began to plot the monthly average lost workdays. After six months of plotting the average lost workdays as they were occurring, the safety man-ager found that the points were all well above the upper control limit. Going back through the three years of data used to construct the chart, the safety manager no-ticed a jump in the severity of injuries after a new production line operation was added to the production department two years earlier. Identifying this new production line as a significant change in the department, it was decided to recalculate the control chart using data collected after the introduction of the new line.

Attribute Control Charts

Attribute charts are used when the data being measured meet certain conditions or attributes. Attributes are involved when the safety measures are categorical (Griffin 2000, 434). Examples of categorical data include the departments in which accidents are occurring, the job classification of the injured employee, and the type of injury sustained. The type of attribute control chart used depends on the data format of the specific attribute measured. The attribute charts covered in this chapter are

- p-chart, for controlling the number of nonconformities; used with binomial data.
- u-chart, for controlling the number of nonconformities per unit of exposure; used with Poisson process data.

- c-chart, for controlling the number of nonconformities; used with data from samples of various sizes.
- np-chart, for controlling the number of nonconformities.

p-Chart

The *p-chart* is used with "binomial" data—or data with two possible outcomes. For example, a p-chart may be used to chart the percentage of each sample that is non-conforming to the safety requirements (Juran and Godfrey 1999, 45.12). P-charts have the advantage of taking into account the sample size (e.g., the number of work orders completed) and accounting for the high level of random fluctuations when the sample size is small (e.g., very few workers exposed). P-charts can also be used when the subgroups are not of equal size.

The control limits for the p-chart are normally expressed in terms of the standard deviation. The formula for calculating the standard deviation is (Juran and Godfrey 1999, 45.12):

$$\sigma = \sqrt{\frac{p(1-p)}{n}}$$

Where:
- σ is the standard deviation
- p   is the percentage of nonconformities
- n   is the total number of subjects

So the upper and lower control limits for a p-chart will be at:

$$\overline{p} \pm 3 \sqrt{\frac{\overline{p}(1-\overline{p})}{n}}$$

Where:

- $\overline{p}$ is the mean percentage of nonconformities
- n   is the number of subjects in each sample

As a general rule of thumb, when constructing the control chart, a minimum of 20 to 25 sample periods should be collected over a sufficient period of time (Juran and Godfrey 1999, 45.13). Within each of those samples, the number of observations needs to be large enough to have defects present in the subgroup most of the time. For example, suppose a safety manager collects 3 accident reports for a month's sample to determine the extent of the back injury problem. Three accident reports may not be a large enough number of observations to identify a back injury problem in the plant. Had the safety manager selected more accident forms for analysis, a back injury problem may have been identified. The question for the safety manager is "How many observations should one take in a sample?" One of the ways to estimate how many observations should be taken in a sample is to use the historical rates. If we have some idea as to the historical rate of nonconformance, p, we can use the following formula to estimate the subgroup size:

$$n = \frac{3}{p}$$

Where:
    n   represents the sample size
    p   represents the proportion of nonconformities

Another problem that safety managers are faced with is that the number of observations in the samples may not be equal. If the subgroup size (n) varies, there are three possibilities that can be used to construct the p-chart (Juran and Godfrey 1999, 45.13):

1. We can calculate the average size of the subgroups. This is appropriate when the sizes are similar or all data lie near the centerline.

2. We can calculate separate control limits for each subgroup. However, this might lead to a confusing chart.

3. We can find the average of the subgroup size and use the resulting control limits, but when a point falls near of the control limit, calculate the actual limits using the actual subgroup size.

The average for the p control chart is the overall average fraction for the sample.

Sample p-Chart

Data were collected for all reported injuries during a 10-week period. The safety manager wished to construct a control chart depicting the percentage of reported injuries that were hand injuries. The following table was constructed:

Week Number	Number of Reports	Number of Hand Injuries	Fraction of Hand Injuries
1	152	5	0.0329
2	103	6	0.0583
3	75	4	0.0533
4	128	6	0.0469
5	90	5	0.0556
6	174	7	0.0402
7	144	4	0.0278
8	167	9	0.0539
9	108	7	0.0648
10	119	6	0.0504
Totals	1260	59	
Averages	126	5.9	0.0484

The upper and lower control limits for a p-chart will be at:

$$\overline{p} \pm 3 \sqrt{\frac{\overline{p}(1-\overline{p})}{n}}$$

$$UCL = .0484 + 3 \sqrt{\frac{.0484(1-.0484)}{126}} = .1054$$

$$LCL = .0484 - 3 \sqrt{\frac{.0484(1-.0484)}{126}} = -.0086$$

Where:

    $\overline{p}$ is the mean percentage of nonconformities

    p   is the percentage of nonconformities

    n   is the number of subjects in each sample

    UCL is the Upper Control Limit

    LCL is the Lower Control Limit

The control chart for the data set would be as depicted in Figure 4.4.

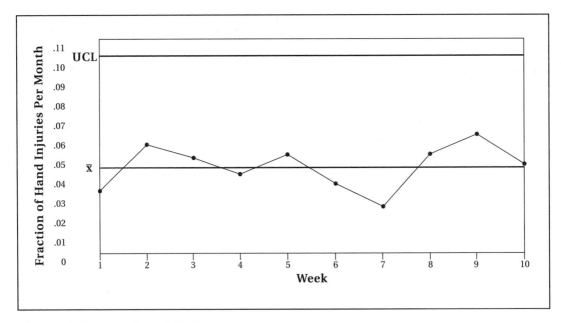

Figure 4.4. Sample p-Chart

Interpreting the p-Chart

Data selected over the 10-week period was used to construct the p-chart that appears in Figure 4.4. Examination of the chart indicates that the data used in the construction of the chart is considered to be in control since the plotted points consistently fall between the upper and lower control limits and the data points do not meet any of the criteria for an "out-of-control" chart. If and when the data used to construct the chart is out of control, the outliers need to be identified and the reasons for the problem data need to be addressed. A new control chart needs to be constructed with data that is considered in control. With the control chart constructed, the safety manager now collects data in the future and continues to plot the new sample values as they are obtained in the future. Evaluations and interpretations are made as new data points are added to the chart in terms of out-of-control data or the need to recalculate the control chart to narrow the control limits.

c-Chart

The *c-chart* is used for "Poisson" processes. This type of chart monitors the number of relatively infrequent "events" in each of many equal samples (constant sample size). For example, occurrence-reporting data (i.e., number of accidents per month) are usually plotted on c-charts because the data empirically appears to fit the "Poisson" model.

The standard deviation for a c-chart is (Juran and Godfrey 1999):

$$\sigma = \sqrt{\bar{c}}$$

where $\bar{c}$ is the average number of nonconformities per unit of time. (In this case, the "unit," commonly referred to as an *inspection unit,* is a standard measure of time—usually something such as "per month.") The upper and lower control limits for a c-chart will be at:

$$\bar{c} \pm 3\sqrt{\bar{c}}$$

Sample c-Chart

Data were collected for a 12-month period from accident reports. The safety manager wished to construct a control chart depicting the frequency of back injuries reported each month. The following table was constructed:

Month	Number of Back Injuries
1	1
2	0
3	0
4	2
5	1
6	0
7	0
8	0
9	2
10	3
11	4
12	3
Totals	16
Average Number of Back Injuries per Month	1.33

The upper control limit for the c-chart will be at:

$$1.33 + 3\sqrt{1.33} = 4.79$$

The lower control limit for the c-chart will be at:

$$1.33 - 3\sqrt{1.33} = -2.13$$

Since a value of -2.13 is not achievable, the lower control limit should be set to 0. The resulting control chart is in Figure 4.5.

Examination of this chart indicates that the data used in the construction of the chart is considered to be in control since the plotted points consistently fall between the upper and lower control limits and the data points do not meet any of the criteria for an "out-of-control" chart. With the control chart constructed, the safety manager now collects data in the future and continues to plot the new sample values as they are obtained in the future adding the points to the chart. As the new samples are plotted, the safety manager evaluates the data in the same manner as described in the previous control charts.

u-Chart

The *u-chart* can be used when counting accidents per sample when the sample size varies for each observation (Training Resources and Data Exchange [TRADE] 1995). U-charts are used when it is not possible to have an inspection unit of a fixed size. This chart is also referred to as a standardized chart (Juran and Godfrey 1999). A good example of data suited to this chart is the number of lost or restricted workday cases

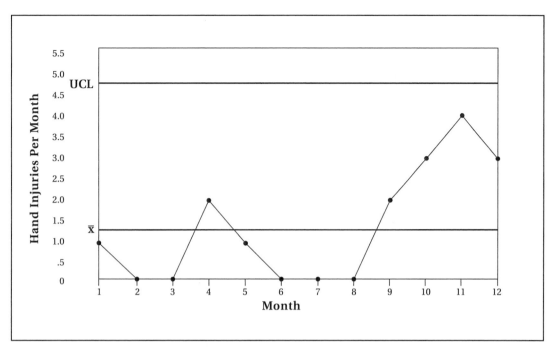

Figure 4.5. Sample c-Chart

per 200,000 man-hours. In this case, the number of cases is counted in fixed time intervals (that is, the records provide data on the number of cases per month), but the sample size used (the number of man-hours worked during each month) changes.

The standard deviation is calculated using the average number of nonconformities per unit of measure ($\overline{u}$) and the average sample size per measurement ($\overline{n}$). The formula used to calculate the standard deviation is:

$$\sigma = \sqrt{\frac{\overline{u}}{\overline{n}}}$$

The upper and lower control limits for a u chart are set by (Juran and Godfrey 1999):

$$\overline{u} \pm 3 \sqrt{\frac{\overline{u}}{\overline{n}}}$$

Sample u-Chart

OSHA recordable injury incidence rates were collected for a 12-month period. The risk manager wished to construct a control chart depicting the incidence rates for each month. The following table was constructed:

Month	Man Hours Worked	Recordable Injuries	Injury Rate
1	5,700	3	0.0005
2	5,600	4	0.0007
3	5,500	3	0.0005
4	5,400	2	0.0004
5	5,600	4	0.0007
6	5,000	5	0.0010
7	5,600	3	0.0005
8	5,500	2	0.0004
9	5,400	4	0.0007
10	5,600	5	0.0009
11	5,500	2	0.0004
12	5,400	2	0.0004
Totals	65,800	39	

The average number of nonconformities ($\bar{u}$) is:

$$\bar{u} = 39/65,800 = .0006$$

The average number sample size ($\bar{n}$) is:

$$\bar{n} = 65,800/12 = 5,483.3$$

The upper control limit for the u-chart will be at:

$$.0006 + 3\sqrt{\frac{.0006}{5,483.3}} = .0016$$

The lower control limit for the u-chart will be at:

$$.0006 - 3\sqrt{\frac{.0006}{5,483.3}} = -.0004$$

The completed control chart appears in Figure 4.6.

An alternative to using the overall average number of man-hours worked is to calculate the upper and lower control limits using the number of man-hours worked for that specific month. This method would result in moving upper and lower control limits. It is preferred to calculate the control limits month to month when there is a difference of 25% or more in the sample sizes. In the following example, data was collected on the number of first-aid cases resulting from the use of a production process in a manufacturing facility. The number of days per month in which the production line was used varies from month to month. This variation exceeds a 25% difference from one month to another. Therefore, the safety manager has decided to calculate the control limits from month to month. The same formula is used for calculating the average. However, when calculating the upper and lower control limits, the number of units (in this case, the number of times the production line operated) is used for

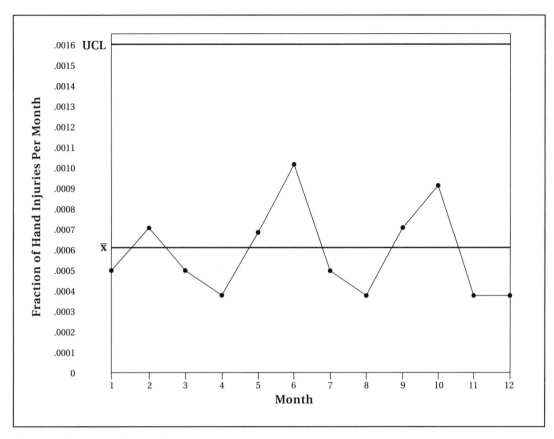

Figure 4.6 Sample u-Chart

Month	Number of times the production line was run	Number of first aid cases	First Aid Case Rate per line run	UCL	LCL
1	5	0	0	1.27	0 (-.45)
2	7	4	.57	1.14	0 (-.32)
3	9	5	.56	1.05	0 (-.23)
4	4	2	.50	1.37	0 (-.55)
5	7	3	.43	1.14	0 (-.32)
6	6	2	.33	1.19	0 (-.37)
7	3	0	0	1.52	0 (-.70)
8	7	5	.71	1.14	0 (-.32)
9	9	4	.44	1.05	0 (-.23)
10	5	1	.20	1.27	0 (-.45)
11	4	1	.25	1.37	0 (-.55)
12	8	3	.38	1.09	0 (-.32)
Totals	74	30			

each month rather than the average number of times the production line operated for the entire period.

The average number of first-aid cases per production line used ($\bar{u}$) is $30/74 = .41$. The upper control limit for Period 1 is $.41 + 3\sqrt{.41/5} = 1.27$, and the lower control limit is $.41 - 3\sqrt{.41/5} = -.44$ (indicated as 0 on the chart since the obtained value is negative). This same process is followed for each period under observation. The control chart using this technique appears in Figure 4.7.

This chart indicates that the data used in its construction is considered to be in control. As is the case with out-of-control data, the reasons for the problem data need to be addressed, and a new control chart needs to be constructed. The safety manager now collects new data and continues to plot the new sample values as they are obtained in the future. As new data is collected, it is plotted and analyzed.

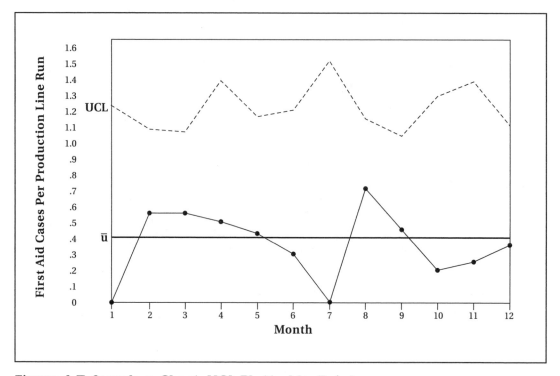

Figure 4.7. Sample u-Chart, UCL Plotted by Point

np-Charts

Like p-charts, *np-charts* are used to analyze accidents and other "nonconforming events" or "deviations" over a constant period; however, the np-chart uses a constant sample size and plots the *number* of nonconformities (np) rather than the *percentage* of nonconformities (p) (Griffin, p. 439). The steps to follow for constructing an np-chart are the same as for a p-chart (Training Resources and Data Exchange (TRADE) 1995, 2-1). The np-chart is used when:

1. The number of defectives is easier or more meaningful to report.
2. The sample size (n) remains constant from period to period.

The upper and lower control limits for a np-chart can be derived by (Juran and Godfrey 1999, 45.14):

$$n\bar{p} \pm 3\sqrt{n\bar{p}(1-\bar{p})}$$

where $n\bar{p}$ is equal to the average number of nonconformities per group and $\bar{p}$ is equal to the average fraction of nonconformities per group. An alternative method for calculating the upper and lower control limits for an np-chart is (Juran and Godfrey 1999, 45.15):

$$\bar{x} \pm 3\sqrt{\bar{x}\left(\frac{1-\bar{x}}{n}\right)}$$

Where $\bar{x}$ is equal to the average number of nonconformities per group and n is equal to the number of items in each subgroup.

Sample np-Chart

In the following example, data was collected over five day observation periods in which the number of hand injuries was identified. The first step in constructing the control chart is to determine the average number of hand injuries per analysis period ($n\bar{p}$). Since there are 5 observations per group (n), multiplying the proportion of hand injuries for the group (p) yields the number of injuries. Therefore, $n\bar{p}$ is equal to the average number of cases per observation group for the analysis period ($.28 \times 5 = 1.4$). This number can also be obtained by calculating the average number of hand injuries for the analysis period (14 injuries / 10 periods = 1.4). With $n\bar{p}$ calculated, the upper and lower control limits can be derived using the formula provided. The example in the next section illustrates how the upper and lower control limits are calculated.

Week Number	Number of days (N)	Number of Hand Injuries	Fraction of Hand Injuries
1	5	2	0.4
2	5	1	0.2
3	5	1	0.2
4	5	0	0.0
5	5	0	0.0
6	5	2	0.4
7	5	3	0.6
8	5	1	0.2
9	5	2	0.4
10	5	2	0.4
Totals	50	14	

The average number of injuries per 5-day period is 1.4. The number in each subgroup (n) is constant at 5. The upper control limit would be calculated as:

$$1.4 + 3\sqrt{1.4\left(\frac{1-1.4}{5}\right)} = 4.41$$

The lower control limit would be calculated as:

$$1.4 - 3\sqrt{1.4\left(\frac{1-1.4}{5}\right)} = -1.61$$

Since the lower control limit, -1.61, is unattainable, the lower control limit should be set to 0. The sample np chart appears in Figure 4.8.

This chart indicates that the data used in its construction is considered to be in control. As is the case with out of control data, the reasons for the problem data need to be addressed and a new control chart needs to be constructed. The safety manager now collects data in the future and continues to plot the new sample values as they are obtained in the future. As new data is collected, it is plotted and analyzed.

Variables Control Charts

Control charts based on measurements of quality characteristics are often found to be a more economical means of controlling performance than control charts based on attributes (Duncan 1974, 431). The two most common types of variables control charts are $\bar{x}$-charts and R-charts.

$\bar{x}$-chart

The $\bar{x}$-chart is used primarily with "variable" data, which are usually measurements such as the concentration of hazardous materials in the air, the number of days it

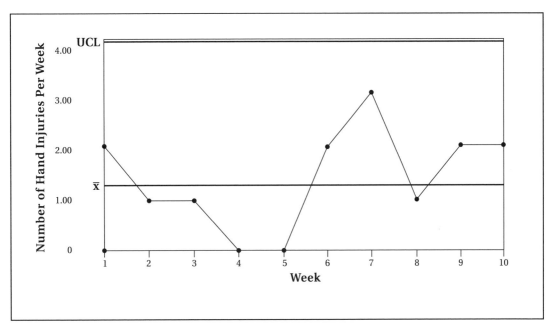

Figure 4.8. Sample np-Chart

takes to return from an accident, or the number of accidents per period. An acceptable method to calculate the standard deviation for an x̄-chart is to calculate the standard deviation for a sample. The formula for calculating the standard deviation is presented in Chapter 3.

The first step in constructing an x̄-chart is to calculate the average of each subgroup and the grand mean of all subgroups using the formula presented in Chapter 3. Next, the upper control limit and the lower control limit can be calculated using the following formulas. (A_2 can be found in the table in Appendix A. An excerpt from the table is presented below.)

$$UCL = \overline{X} + A_2 \overline{R}$$

$$LCL = \overline{X} - A_2 \overline{R}$$

Where:
  UCL is the upper control limit
  LCL is the lower control limit
  $\overline{X}$ is the mean of the measurements
  A_2 is the value taken from the table in Appendix A
  $\overline{R}$ is the mean of the ranges for the measurements (the range is determined by subtracting the highest measurement from the lowest)

The value for A_2 can be found in the following table (also printed in the table in Appendix A):

N	A_2
2	1.880
3	1.023
4	.729
5	.577
6	.483
7	.419
8	.373
9	.337

where N is the number of observations per group.

The data are interpreted using the following guidelines; the process is *not* in control if there are (Juran and Godfrey 1999, 45.10):

a.   One or more points outside the 3 sigma control limits

b.   Eight or more successive points on the same side of the centerline

c.   Six or more successive points that increase or decrease

d.   Two out of three points that are on the same side of the centerline, both at a distance exceeding 2 sigmas from the centerline

e.   Four out of five points that are on the same side of the centerline, four at a distance exceeding 1 sigma from the centerline

$\bar{x}$-Chart Example

The following data consist of 20 sets of three measurements of levels (in ppm) of an air contaminant in the production area of a manufacturing facility.

N	Measurement #1	Measurement #2	Measurement #3	Range	Mean
1	50	48	47	3	48.3
2	51	50	49	2	50.0
3	50	51	50	1	50.3
4	49	50	50	2	49.7
5	48	47	51	3	48.7
6	50	49	48	2	49.0
7	51	50	50	1	50.3
8	50	51	49	2	50.0
9	49	48	47	2	48.0
10	50	50	49	1	49.7
11	51	51	50	1	50.7
12	48	50	50	2	49.3
13	50	47	51	4	49.3
14	50	49	48	2	49.0
15	51	50	50	1	50.3

N	Measurement #1	Measurement #2	Measurement #3	Range	Mean
16	50	51	49	2	50.0
17	49	48	47	2	48.0
18	50	50	49	1	49.7
19	51	51	50	1	50.7
20	48	50	51	3	49.7
Mean				1.9	49.5

To construct an $\bar{x}$-chart, the ranges and the means for each measurement period were calculated. Next, the safety manager calculated the overall mean of all the ranges and the mean of all the means, otherwise referred to as the *grand mean* ($\bar{\bar{X}}$).

$$\bar{\bar{X}} = (48.3 + 50.5 + 50.3 \ldots) / 20 = 49.5$$

The average range ($\bar{R}$) is the average of the ranges. It is calculated as:

$$\bar{R} = (3 + 2 + 1 \ldots) / 20 = 1.9$$

The value for A_2 is obtained from the table in Appendix A. Since there are 3 observations per group (n = 3), the obtained table value is 1.023.

The upper and lower control limits are calculated by (American Society for Testing and Materials 1995):

$$\text{UCL} = \bar{\bar{X}} + A_2 \times \bar{R} = 49.5 + 1.023 \times 1.9 = 51.4$$

$$\text{LCL} = \bar{\bar{X}} - A_2 \times \bar{R} = 49.5 - 1.023 \times 1.9 = 47.6$$

This chart (Figure 4.9) indicates that the data used in its construction is considered to be in control. As is the case with out of control data, the reasons for the problem data need to be addressed and a new control chart needs to be constructed. The safety manager now collects data in the future and continues to plot the new sample values as they are obtained in the future. As new data is collected, it is plotted and analyzed.

R-Chart

R-charts are control charts used to track the ranges of samples. The range of a sample is the difference between the largest observation and the smallest. The range is not recommended for sample sizes greater than 10 since it becomes less effective than the standard deviation as a detector of causes (American Society for Testing and Materials 1995). To construct an R-chart, data are divided into subgroupings of (usually)

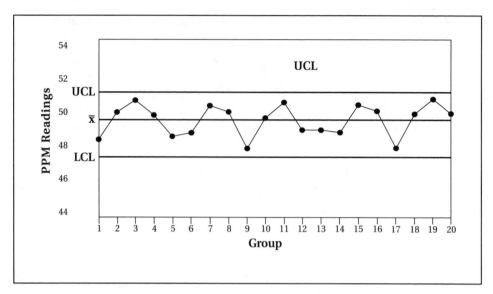

Figure 4.9. Sample $\bar{x}$-Chart

four or five points. The average of each subgroup is plotted on the $\bar{x}$-chart, and the range (the highest value minus the lowest value) is plotted on the R-chart. The standard deviation for each graph is calculated by determining the mean of the range values (signified as $\bar{R}$). First, the R-chart is constructed. If the R-chart validates that the process variation is in statistical control, the $\bar{x}$-chart is constructed.

When constructing an R-chart, make certain there are at least 20 groups and there are between 1 and 9 measurements in each group. There are typically 3 to 5 measurements per group. To find the range of each subgroup, subtract the smallest measurement from the largest. The average range ($\bar{R}$) is the average of the ranges. It is calculated with:

$$\bar{R} = (.0004 + .0005 + .0007 \ldots) / 20 = .0005$$

The upper and lower control limits can be found with the following formulas (American Society for Testing and Materials 1995):

$$UCL = D_4 \bar{R}$$

$$LCL = D_3 \bar{R}$$

Where:
    D_3 is the value from the table in Appendix A
    D_4 is the value from the table in Appendix A

$\overline{R}$ is the average range for the measurements
UCL is the upper control limit
LCL is the lower control limit

D_3 and D_4 can be found in the table in Appendix A. An excerpt from the table follows:

n	D_3	D_4
2	0	3.267
3	0	2.574
4	0	2.282
5	0	2.114
6	0	2.004
7	0.076	1.924
8	0.136	1.864
9	0.184	1.816

Plotting the subgroup data will allow the analyst to determine if the process is in statistical control. If it is not, the subgroups that are identified as being outliers should be eliminated if the cause for their deviation can be explained. A new chart can be reconstructed with the new data. Do not eliminate subgroups with points out of range for which assignable causes cannot be found. Once the R-chart is in a state of statistical control and the centerline $\overline{R}$ can be considered a reliable estimate of the range, the process standard deviation can be estimated using:

$$\sigma = \overline{R} / d_2$$

Where:
   σ is the standard deviation
   d_2 is the table value for d_2
   $\overline{R}$ is the average range for the measurements

The value for d_2 can be found in the table located in Appendix A, using $n=3$ since there are 3 measurements per group. An excerpt from the table follows:

n	d_2
2	1.128
3	1.693
4	2.059
5	2.326
6	2.534
7	2.704
8	2.847
9	2.970

R-Chart Example

Using the same data presented in the $\bar{x}$-chart section of this chapter, an R-chart can be constructed using the ranges obtained in the measurements for each trial. The mean range ($\bar{R}$) is the mean of all ranges. It is calculated as:

$$\bar{R} = (\text{Range Trial \#1} + \text{Range Trial \#2} + \text{Range Trial \#3} \ldots) / \text{Number of Trials}$$

The upper and lower control limits are calculated using the following formulas and table located in Appendix A again using n=3 since there are 3 measurements per group.

$$\text{UCL} = D(4) \times \bar{R} = 2.574 \times 1.9 = 4.8906$$

$$\text{LCL} = D(3) \times \bar{R} = 0.000 \times 1.9 = 0.000$$

R-Chart Sample Data

N	Measurement #1	Measurement #2	Measurement #3	Range	Mean
1	50	48	47	3	48.3
2	51	50	49	2	50.0
3	50	51	50	1	50.3
4	49	50	50	2	49.7
5	48	47	51	3	48.7
6	50	49	48	2	49.0
7	51	50	50	1	50.3
8	50	51	49	2	50.0
9	49	48	47	2	48.0
10	50	50	49	1	49.7
11	51	51	50	1	50.7
12	48	50	50	2	49.3
13	50	47	51	4	49.3
14	50	49	48	2	49.0
15	51	50	50	1	50.3
16	50	51	49	2	50.0
17	49	48	47	2	48.0
18	50	50	49	1	49.7
19	51	51	50	1	50.7
20	48	50	51	3	49.7
Mean				1.9	49.5

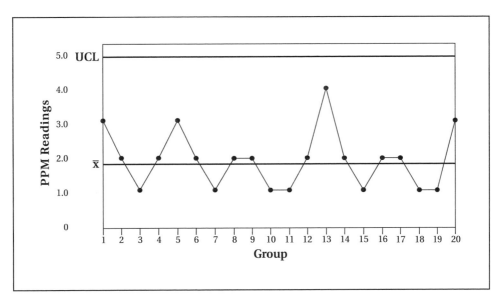

Figure 4.10. Sample R-Chart

s-Chart

The sample standard deviation(s) may be used with the x̄-chart in place of the sample range to measure the process dispersion. When doing so, an s-control chart is constructed. In this case, calculate the sample standard deviations, find the average standard deviations, and calculate the control limits from the following equations (Juran and Godfrey 1999):

UCL = B(4) σ̄

LCL = B(3) σ̄

Where:
    σ̄   is the average standard deviation
    D(2) is the table value for D(2)
    LCL is the lower control limit
    UCL is the upper control limit

The values for B(3) and B(4) can be found in Table 1 of Appendix 1. An excerpt from the table is presented below where n is equal to the number of measurements in each sample:

n	B(3)	B(4)
2	0	3.27
3	0	2.57
4	0	2.27
5	0	2.09
6	.030	1.97
7	0.12	1.88
8	0.19	1.82
9	0.24	1.76

To calculate an s-chart, a minimum of 20 samples of data should be obtained with 1 to 9 measurements in each sample (Juran and Godfrey 1999). The standard deviation for each sample is derived using the standard deviation formula presented in Chapter 3. These standard deviations are then averaged using the formula for calculating a mean. The result is the average standard deviation, $\bar{\sigma}$.

The s-chart is interpreted using the following guidelines to determine if the process is in control (Juran and Godfrey 1999, 45.10):

a. one point outside the 3-sigma control limit

b. two out of three points that are on the same side of the centerline, both at a distance exceeding 2 sigmas from the centerline

c. eight successive points on the same side of the centerline

d. four out of five points that are on the same side of the centerline, four at a distance exceeding 1 sigma from the centerline

e. six successive points that increase or decrease

s-Chart Example

The following data consist of 20 sets of three measurements of air contaminant readings as measured in parts per million (PPM).

n	Measurement #1	Measurement #2	Measurement #3	Standard Deviation
1	50	48	47	1.53
2	51	50	49	1.00
3	50	51	50	0.58
4	49	50	50	0.58
5	48	47	51	2.08
6	50	49	48	1.00
7	51	50	50	0.58
8	50	51	49	1.00
9	49	48	47	1.00

n	Measurement #1	Measurement #2	Measurement #3	Standard Deviation
10	50	50	49	0.58
11	51	51	50	0.58
12	48	50	50	1.15
13	50	47	51	2.08
14	50	49	48	1.00
15	51	50	50	0.58
16	50	51	49	1.00
17	49	48	47	1.00
18	50	50	49	0.58
19	51	51	50	0.58
20	48	50	51	1.53
Average				1.00

The upper and lower control limits for an s-chart are calculated as follows:

$\bar{\sigma} = 1.00$

$UCL = B(4) \times \bar{\sigma} = 2.568 \times 1.00 = 2.568$

$LCL = B(3) \times \bar{\sigma} = 0 \times 1.00 = 0$

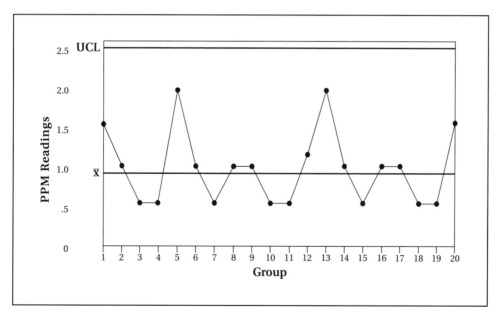

Figure 4.11. Sample s-Chart

Pareto Charts

Vilfredo Pareto was a nineteenth-century economist who studied the distribution of wealth and income. Most of the wealth at this time was concentrated in a few hands, and the great majority of people were in poverty. The Pareto Principle states that in any population that contributes to a common effect, a relative few of the contributors account for the bulk of the effect (Juran and Godfrey 1999).

Pareto Diagram Analysis

Pareto Analysis is used to identify and evaluate the factors that contribute to the greatest frequency of unwanted events. To establish a Pareto Diagram, information about the factors that contribute to the safety problems under analysis must be understood. All contributing factors should be included in the diagram, and therefore the categories should account for 100 percent of the accidents in the investigation. To set up the diagram, determine the frequency of accidents in each category as well as the percentage of accidents each category represents. Next, arrange the categories from left to right in descending order based upon the frequency of accidents in that category. In other words, the category with the greatest number of accidents is placed first (on the left), then the category with the second greatest number of accidents is placed next to the first, etc., until all the categories have been placed side by side, in descending order.

The frequency of cases is presented on the left vertical axis while the cumulative percentage of accident cases is presented along the right vertical axis. A bar graph is drawn along the horizontal axis with each category represented by a bar. The heights of the bars are determined by the frequency of cases in that category and the vertical axis along the right hand side of the chart.

Finally, a line graph is also drawn on the chart representing the cumulative percentage of the categories as you move from left to right. The cumulative percentage is derived by adding the percentage of cases from the first category to the percentage of cases in the second category, then the percentage of case from the first and second categories to the percentage of cases in the third, and so on.

The analysis of a Pareto Diagram involves the evaluation of the categories that represent the greatest frequency of cases. From a safety standpoint, the Pareto Diagram Analysis will aid in identifying those situations that result in the greatest number of accidents, keeping in mind that high frequencies do not mean the greatest in terms of severity.

Pareto Chart Example

In the example given in figure 4.12, the frequency of injuries were classified according to the body part affected. Over this period, backs accounted for 40 percent of all injuries, hands accounted for 30 percent, arms accounted for 20 percent and all other injuries accounted for 10 percent. To construct a Pareto diagram, the category that accounted for the greatest percentage of cases is placed to the left of the diagram and the remaining categories are arranged in descending order of overall percentage of injuries. A line is constructed that indicates the cumulative percentage of injures. For example, the first two categories of injuries (back injuries and hand injuries) account for 70 percent of the injuries, so a point is placed at the 70 percent mark. The first three categories account for 90 percent, and so on. All categories in the chart will total to 100 percent of the injuries, and a point with a connecting line is located at the 100 percent mark on the graph.

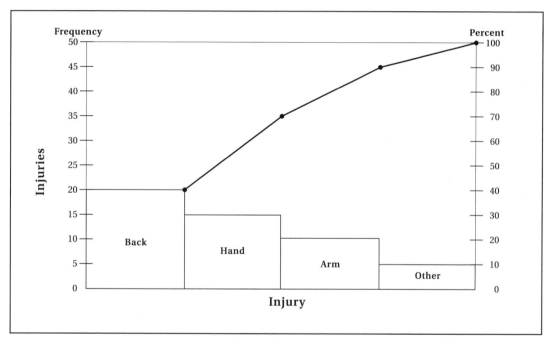

Figure 4.12. Sample Pareto Diagram

Cause and Effect Analysis

Cause and effect analysis is useful in any kind of process capability analysis, not just as the result of attributes inspection and Pareto analysis. The focus of cause and effect analysis is on attacking a problem rather than on fixing blame. Once a nonconformity has been isolated for further study, attention shifts to analyzing how the deviation from specifications was caused. Sometimes the reason is obvious; sometimes a considerable amount of investigation is required to uncover the cause or causes. The Japanese have developed and used cause and effect analysis, and the resulting diagram, as a formal structure for uncovering problem areas. The steps in a cause and effect analysis are (Ishikawa 1982, 18):

1. Determine the quality characteristic. Pareto diagrams can be used to identify the characteristic one would like to improve.
2. Determine the main factors that may be causing lower than expected levels of the quality characteristic. Main factors can be identified through data analysis (i.e., highest frequencies), job analyses, etc.
3. On each branch item, or main factor, determine the detailed factors. Defining and linking the relationships of the possible causal factors should lead to the source of the quality characteristic.

There are various methods for arranging cause and effect diagrams. These methods can be divided into the three following types (Ishikawa 1982, 21):

1. Dispersion Analysis Type: Determines why the dispersion exists
2. Production Process Classification Type: Diagram's main line follows the production process
3. Cause Enumeration Type: All possible causes are listed using brainstorming techniques.

Cause and Effect Analysis Example

An example of a cause and effect analysis chart is depicted in Figure 4.13. In this analysis, the focus was to determine those factors that resulted in over-exposure to hazardous chemicals in the workplace. Using this as the characteristic that needs improvement, the major factors that contributed to the exposure to chemicals were identified. In this example, those factors included poor supervision, lack of personal protective equipment, unsafe job procedures, and a lack of engineering controls. Each of these factors is represented by an arrow feeding into the main horizontal arrow. For each of these major contributing factors, additional factors were identified that contribute to the main causal factor. For example, the lack of personal protective equipment was due primarily to the fact that the hazards were not properly assessed. This was indicated on the cause and effect chart by an arrow feeding into the "Lack of PPE" arrow. When completed, this chart represents those factors that contribute to the unwanted situation. Prevention strategies can then be formulated that address the factors identified in the chart.

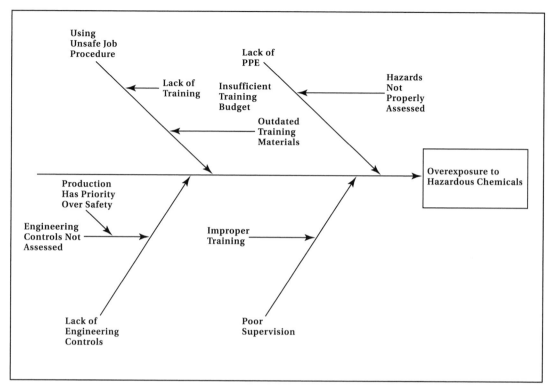

Figure 4.13. Cause and Effect Diagram

Summary

Safety managers often use control charts and run charts to monitor safety performance in the workplace and identify trends that may signify a problem (much in the same way an engineer monitors a production process for potential problems). Although the safety manager is not measuring product defects, accidents, losses, and property damage can be monitored and examined through the use of control charts in the same manner.

Because of the underlying statistical processes used with control charts, the safety manager can identify safety performance problems when they become statistically significant. The safety manager can also use control charts to implement continual improvement programs related to safety activities.

Chapter Questions

1. Differentiate between a run chart and a control chart.
2. Define the following: x-axis, y-axis, UCL, LCL.
3. What is a "run down of 6" mean for a control chart?
4. What does it mean when a control chart is "out of control?"
5. If there is a significant change identified on a control chart, what action can be taken?
6. Describe the uses for p, u, c and np charts?
7. Describe the uses for r, x and s charts?
8. What is a common number of standard deviations used to signify upper and lower control limits?
9. The following data was obtained from CJD Industries:

n	Measurement #1	Measurement #2	Measurement #3
1	50	48	47
2	51	50	49
3	50	51	50
4	49	50	50
5	48	47	51
6	50	49	48
7	51	50	50
8	50	51	49
9	49	48	47
10	50	50	49
11	51	51	50
12	48	50	50
13	50	47	51
14	50	49	48
15	51	50	50
16	50	51	49
17	49	48	47
18	50	50	49
19	51	51	50
20	48	50	51
Average			

Develop an "s chart" for the data.

10. What is a Pareto diagram and Pareto Analysis used to identify?

5

Trending and Forecasting

The concepts of trending and forecasting are used extensively in safety performance measurement. Forecasting accidental losses or any other future event requires detecting past patterns and projecting them into the future (Tiller, Blinn, Kelly, and Head 1989, 23). There are often important, constant elements to these patterns: the frequency of work injuries may be predictably related to output levels, the rate at which inflation increases the financial impact of a given injury may continue past inflationary trends, etc. (Tiller, Blinn, Kelly, and Head 1989, 24). Thus, forecasting future losses by finding these patterns begins with deciding which of two basic patterns, "no change" or "change in a predictable way," applies. Under "no change" patterns, probability analysis is particularly appropriate for forecasting losses; under "change in a predictable way," regression analysis is the better choice (Tiller, Blinn, Kelly, and Head 1989, 24).

Correlations

Correlation procedures are used indicate a measure of association (i.e., some relationship between two or more variables (Horvath 1974, 252). If the correlation procedure uses two variables, the correlation is said to be bivariate. In a bivariate correlation, one variable is identified as the independent variable and the other the dependent variable. The independent variable is that which one cannot change or influence while the dependent variable is the characteristic that is influenced by the independent variable. For example, a safety manager wishes to examine the relationship between the number of hours of training attended and the number of accidents reported in a year for employees in a department. For each employee, or subject, the number of hours of training attended is collected and the number of accidents reported. In this example, the independent variable is the number of hours of training attended and the dependent variable is the number of accidents reported. The safety manager reaches this conclusion because it is the number of hours of training that is expected to influence the number of accidents reported. One would not expect the number of accidents reported to influence the number of hours of training a person attends. When calculating correlations, the independent variable is indicated as the "x" variable and the dependent variable the "y" variable.

The value of a correlation procedure, signified by r or the correlation coefficient, falls along a continuum between -1.00 and $+1.00$ with 0 being the midpoint. As the correlation approaches -1.00 or $+1.00$, the strength of the relationship increases. As the value of the correlation coefficient approaches 0, the strength of the relationship weakens. With a correlation of 1.00, referred to as a perfect correlation, for every change in the value of the dependent variable, there is an identical change in the dependent variable's value. Along the ends of the continuum of correlation coefficients, negative correlations are considered inverse relationships and positive correlation coefficients are considered positive relationships. In an inverse relationship, as the value of the independent variable increases in value, the dependent variable decreases in value. In a positive correlation, as the value of the independent variable increases in value, the value of the dependent variable increases.

A scatterplot is used to graphically represent data points in a correlation procedure. The axes of a scatterplot are arranged so that the values of the independent variable are plotted along the horizontal axis (x axis) and the values for the dependent variable are plotted along the vertical axis (y axis). A data point on the scatterplot represents each subject. The placement of points on a scatterplot is achieved by locating the value of the subject's independent variable along the x-axis and the value of their dependent variable along the vertical axis (y-axis). The point at which the two values intersect on the scatterplot is the location where the point is placed representing that subject. The same process is followed for all subjects for which the correlation will be calculated.

Scatterplots graphically provide a representation of the correlation in terms of the strength and direction (inverse relationship versus positive). Scatterplot A represents a positive correlation. As the values along the horizontal axis increase, the corresponding values on the vertical axis also increase. Scatterplot B on the other hand represents a negative or inverse relationship. As the values on the horizontal axis increase, the corresponding values on the vertical axis decrease.

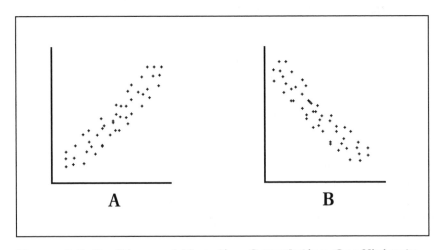

Figure 5.1. Positive and Negative Correlation Coefficients

Scatterplots can also be used to depict the strength of the correlation or relationship between two variables. As the correlation coefficient nears 0, it is referred to as "no correlation" or "no relationship." The points on a scatterplot tend to appear as a cloud without a real pattern toward either a positive or a negative correlation. In Figure 5.2, scatterplot A represents a weak correlation.

Moving away from the 0 in either direction, the strength of the association increases. As the points on a scatterplot approach a straight line, the correlation coefficient approaches 1.00. Scatterplot B represents a strong negative correlation. Scatterplots that range between a perfectly straight line and a circular cloud can then represent correlations between 0 and 1.00. Scatterplot C can depict a moderate positive correlation.

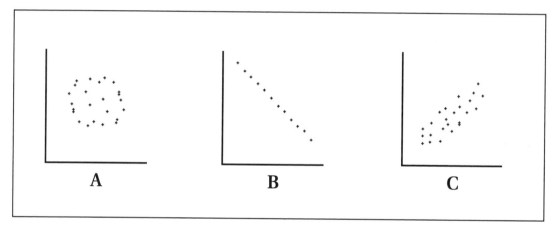

A   B   C

Figure 5.2. Strengths of the Correlation Coefficients

Another measure for the correlation coefficient is the r^2. Squaring the correlation coefficient gives the researcher an indication of the amount of variability in the dependent variable that can be directly attributed to the independent variable. This is referred to as the coefficient of determination. For example, if a correlation coefficient of .75 was obtained from a correlation procedure, then $.75^2$ or 56% of the variability in the dependent variable can be attributed to the independent variable.

Pearson Correlation Coefficient

The Pearson Correlation Coefficient can be used to determine if a relationship exists between two variables—both of which are continuous in nature. Examples of safety performance data that can be analyzed can include the number of lost workdays for an injured employee and the years of experience on the job, the concentrations of hazardous materials in the air, and the number of visits to the nurses office, etc. In addition to the requirement for both variables to be continuous, the following additional assumptions must be met in order to use Pearson Correlation coefficient (Horvath 1974, 255–56):

> Each case is independent of one another.
>
> Each variable assumes a normal distribution.
>
> Each variable is measured on either an interval scale or ratio scale.

Pearson Correlation Coefficient Procedure Formula

The following formula is used to calculate the Pearson Correlation Coefficient (Kuzma 1992, 200):

$$r = \frac{\sum xy - \frac{(\sum x)(\sum y)}{N}}{\sqrt{\left[\sum x^2 - \frac{(\sum x)^2}{N}\right]\left[\sum y^2 - \frac{(\sum y)^2}{N}\right]}}$$

Where:

r represents the Pearson Correlation Coefficient

$\sum xy$ represents the sum of the product of the value for each y variable multiplied by the value for each x variable

$\sum x$ the sum of the x variables

$\sum y$ the sum of the y variables

N the number of subjects in the sample

Pearson Correlation Coefficient Sample Problem

The safety manager for CJD Package Delivery wishes to determine if there is a relationship between the number of traffic accidents reported in month by delivery personnel and the number of deliveries made to Big City, USA. Over the past 12 months data was collected to determine this. Since it is hypothesized that the number of deliveries to Big City influences the number of accidents, the number of trips is the independent variable (X) and the number of accidents is the dependent variable (Y). The data obtained is as follows:

Month	Number of Accidents Reported (Y)	Y^2	Number of Trips to Big City, USA (X)	X^2	XY
January	3	9	1	1	3
February	6	36	4	16	24
March	2	4	0	0	0
April	4	16	1	1	4
May	7	49	2	4	14
June	5	25	2	4	10

Month	Number of Accidents Reported (Y)	Y²	Number of Trips to Big City, USA (X)	X²	XY
July	9	81	6	36	54
August	2	4	0	0	0
September	4	16	3	9	12
October	5	25	2	4	10
November	11	121	7	49	77
December	3	9	1	1	3
Total	61	395	29	125	211

Putting the numbers into the above formula, we get:

$$r = \frac{211 - \dfrac{(29)(61)}{12}}{\sqrt{\left[125 - \dfrac{(29)^2}{12}\right]\left[395 - \dfrac{(61)^2}{12}\right]}} = .93$$

Results indicate there is a strong positive relationship (r = .93) between the number of accidents and the number of monthly trips made to Big City, USA.

Determining if the Correlation Coefficient is Significant

When the correlation coefficient calculated, the next step in determining whether a relationship exists between the two variables is to determine if the value for the correlation coefficient is significantly different from zero (the "no relationship" value). To test whether the correlation coefficient is significantly different from zero, a t-test is performed. The following formula is used to calculate t:

$$t = \frac{r}{\sqrt{\dfrac{1 - r^2}{n - 2}}}$$

$$df = n - 2$$

Where:

t   is the t-test value
r   is the correlation coefficient
n   is the number of cases from which the correlation was calculated
df   represents the degrees of freedom

To perform a t-test on a correlation coefficient, one must determine the probability of being correct when concluding that the correlation coefficient is significant. This degree of chance or probability is referred to as the alpha level. A commonly used alpha level in statistics is .05. With an alpha level (a) of .05, there is a 5% chance of being wrong when concluding that the correlation coefficient obtained is significant.

With the correlation coefficient calculated, the t-test is performed using the formula above. When one tests correlation coefficients, one is testing the hypothesis that the coefficient is significantly different from 0—in other words, that a relationship between the X and Y variables really does exist. Using the traffic accident data from the previous example, the safety manager wishes to determine if the correlation coefficient is significant and accept a 5% chance of being wrong. The first step is to calculate the t-test:

$$t = \frac{.93}{\sqrt{\dfrac{1-.93^2}{12-2}}} = 8.00$$

The next step is to determine if the obtained t-test value of 8.00 is significant. This is done by using a t-table which can be found in any basic statistics book. To use the t-table, the degrees of freedom are calculated. In this case, the degrees of freedom are $10 (12-2=10)$. With the t-table, locate the column for $\alpha = .05$ and degrees of freedom (d.f.) $= 10$. The table for a two-tailed test indicates a value of 2.23. Since our obtained t-test value of 8.00 is greater than the table value, we can conclude that there is a significant correlation between the number of traffic accidents and the number of trips to Big City, USA.

Regression

Regression (or "trend") analysis can be used to identify patterns of change in loss frequency or severity that may tend to move together with changes in some other variable (such as time). These patterns can then be used to forecast future experiences (Tiller, Blinn, Kelly, and Head 1989, 34).

Regression procedures allow a person to develop equations that can be used to predict the values of dependent variables from independent variables. In other words, they allow a person to predict the number of injuries, near incidents, etc. (dependent variables), from more certain and easily calculated variables such as time on the job, worker training, etc. (independent variables). In a regression procedure in which losses are correlated with time, the losses are considered the dependent variable since they are influenced as time progresses, and time is considered the independent variable.

Before a regression equation can be developed, a correlation coefficient is first derived. Then an equation for the line that best fits the data points is calculated. The formula for the line that describes the regression is given by:

$$y = bx + a$$

Where:
  b is the slope of the line
  a is the y intercept for the line

As is in correlations, "x" represents the independent variable and "y" represents the dependent variable. The slope of the line is the rise of the line over the run. In order to predict a new "y" variable from an "x", plug the x into the equation and calculate the expected y.

Figure 5.3 represents an equation for the line of $y=.83x+5$. The slope of the line is indicated by the fact that for every increase of 5 in y, there is a 6-step increase in x (in other words, a slope of $5/6=.83$). The line intersects the y-axis at 5, therefore the value for a is 5. To use the equation, one can plug values in for x to determine the expected value for y. For example, to determine the expected value of y for someone that obtains a score of 6 on the x measure, plugging into the equation yields:

$y=.83 (6)+5=10.0$ (see Figure 5.3).

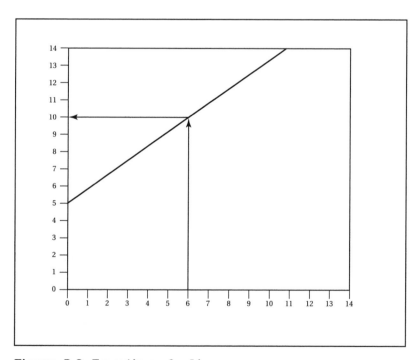

Figure 5.3. Equation of a Line

Procedure Assumptions

The assumptions for the regression are the same for those for Pearson Correlation Coefficient:

Each case is independent of one another.

Each variable assumes a normal distribution.

Each variable is measured on at least the interval scale or ratio scale.

Procedure Formulas

The following formulas are used to calculate the equation of a line, $y = ax + b$ (Cohen and Cohen 1983, 41–43):

$$a = \frac{r \, Sdy}{Sdx}$$

$$b = \overline{Y} - a\overline{X}$$

Where:
  r   = Pearson Correlation Coefficient
  Sdx = Standard deviation of x
  Sdy = Standard deviation of y
  $\overline{X}$ = mean of X
  $\overline{Y}$ = mean of Y

Regression Sample Problem

Using the data from the traffic accidents and number of monthly trips to Big City, USA, the safety manager now wishes to perform a regression procedure on the data. To do so, a Pearson Correlation Coefficient is calculated and tested for significance using the t-test as was done in the previous sections. Those procedures yielded a significant correlation coefficient ($r = .93$, $t = 8.00$). The regression procedure should only be used after a significant correlation has been established. The purpose of the regression is to be able to predict future outcomes—if a significant relationship between the variables has not been established, using the variables to predict future outcomes would be pointless. Using the traffic accident data, the following is performed:

Calculate the standard deviation for the X variable and the Y variable using the methodology presented earlier in the book. The standard deviation for X = 2.24 and the standard deviation for Y = 2.87.

Calculate the means for X and Y using the methodology presented earlier in the book. The mean for X=2.23 and the mean for Y=3.60.

Calculate the term "a" for the equation of a line using the using the methodology presented in this chapter.

$$a = \frac{.93 \times 2.87}{2.24} = 1.19$$

Calculate the term "b" for the equation of a line using the using the methodology presented in this chapter.

$$b = 3.60 - (1.19 \times 2.23) = .95$$

The equation for the line in this regression problem is:

$$y = 1.19x + .95$$

Using this equation, it is now possible to predict future values of Y (number of traffic accidents) given a value for X (number trips to Big City, USA). For example, if there were 20 trips scheduled to Big City, USA next month, how many traffic accidents would one expect to be reported for the month?

$$y = 1.19(20) + .95 = 24.75 \text{ accidents}$$

Summary

Trending and forecasting are common techniques in the insurance industry. However, the ability to accurately predict expected losses is also an extremely useful tool for the safety professional. If one knows where losses and accidents are likely to occur in the future, and to what extent, control measure can be developed and implemented to prevent such occurrences. The tools used in trending and forecasting include correlation procedures, regression, and scatterplots. With the added use of inferential testing of correlation coefficients and the ability to formulate a regression equation, the safety manager has a degree of certainty about the predictions.

Chapter Questions

1. What does a correlation indicate?
2. What is a bivariate correlation?

3. Draw a scatterplot that would be indicative of a strong positive correlation.

4. The following data was obtained from Company CJT. What is the Pearson correlation coefficient?

Case	Fire Losses (Y)	Y^2	Minutes for Fire Brigade to Respond (X)	X^2	XY
1	$100	$10000	15	225	$1500
2	$200	$40000	26	676	$5200
3	$250	$62500	54	2916	$13500
4	$500	$250000	40	1600	$20000
5	$200	$40000	18	324	$3600
Sum	$1250	$402500	153	5741	$43800
Std Dev	$150		16.27		
Average	$250		30.6		

5. A correlation procedure yielded a correlation coefficient of .89. What is the coefficient of determination and what does it represent?

6. What can a regression procedure be used for?

7. If a correlation equation yielded a correlation coefficient of .89 and the standard deviation of X was .18 and the standard deviation of Y was .34, what is the equation of the line?

8. Using the information in Item 7, what would one expect for a value on Y if a value of 6 was obtained for the X variable?

9. How is trending and forecasting used in a safety performance program?

10. What are the data requirements for the Pearson Correlation Procedure?

Effective Data Presentation

Proper presentation of data is an important step in data collection and analysis of safety metrics. Data presentation methods include scatterplots, histograms, tables, pie charts, and line charts. Examples of data that can be presented in the safety field are numerous. They can include the number of injuries, accident rates, exposure levels, safety activity levels, and so on. Proper uses of data presentation techniques include matching the proper presentation format to the proper data format as well as proper design and arrangement of chart and graph components. All of these aid in the proper interpretation and analysis of the data. There are a variety of formats for tables, graphs, and charts, depending upon their uses. One source for table and chart formats is the American Psychological Association which is used by a number of safety journals and publications. Some general guidelines to follow when developing tables, graphs and charts include (American Psychological Association 1995, 140–41):

- The number of main points should be limited in any one table, graph or chart to that which can be easily understood.
- To clearly identify the material, a title that describes the content as to the subject, person, place, and time should always be included. Titles should be numbered.
- The body of the data must be arranged in meaningful intervals.
- The source of the information should always be identified, usually as a footnote.

Scatterplots

A scatterplot is a graph containing a cluster of dots that represents all pairs of observations (Witte and Witte 1997, 132). Each point on a scatterplot represents one case. And the case appears on the plot in relation to its measure on two scales. Both scales on a scatterplot represent variables. The variables used on a scatterplot are continuous in nature, with the independent variable along the horizontal axis (x) and the dependent variable along the vertical (y) axis.

As presented in Chapter 5, scatterplots can be useful in graphically presenting the relationships between the variables plotted. The shape of the plotted data points can show the strength and type of the relationship. When constructing a scatterplot, the divisions along the x and y axes should be uniform and labeled. The plot itself should be labeled in terms of the variables presented and the source of the data. An example of a scatterplot is presented in Figure 6.1.

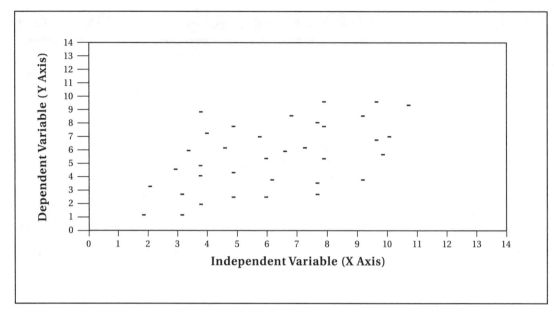

Figure 6.1. Sample Scatterplot

Histograms

Histograms use continuous data and depict continuous scale data for subjects in the sample or population. A histogram has two axes. Along the x-axis, the continuous data measures are indicated. They may be individual scores or groups of scores. If the horizontal scale represents groups of scores, each range must be of equal size. The vertical axis (y axis) represents the frequency of cases in each of the horizontal groups. Characteristics of a well-constructed histogram include (Witte and Witte 1997, 40):

1. Equal units along the horizontal axis (the X axis, or abscissa) reflect the various class intervals of the frequency distribution.

2. Equal units along the vertical axis (the Y axis, or ordinate) reflect increases in frequency. (The units along the vertical axis do not have to be the same size as those along the horizontal axis.)

3. The intersection of the two axes defines the origin at which both weight and frequency equal 0.

4. Numbers always increase from left to right along the horizontal axis and from bottom to top along the vertical axis.

5. The body of the histogram consists of a series of bars whose heights reflect the frequencies for the various class intervals.

6. Adjacent bars in histograms have common boundaries.

Histograms are most often used to display information such as the distribution of scores on a test. In the safety field, a variety of data lends itself well to the histogram, including the distribution of dollar losses due to accidents for an organization, the number of hours of safety training employees have attended, and the number of lost workdays for a particular type of injury. Using the histogram to display this type of information provides the safety manger with a graphical representation of the distribution of the data. The graph can indicate if the data tends to cluster around various points of the distribution or toward one end or the other. Comparisons between histograms can provide the safety manager with information pertaining to any shifts in experience—for example, if there a general decrease in the level of accidental losses experienced by the company from one period to the next.

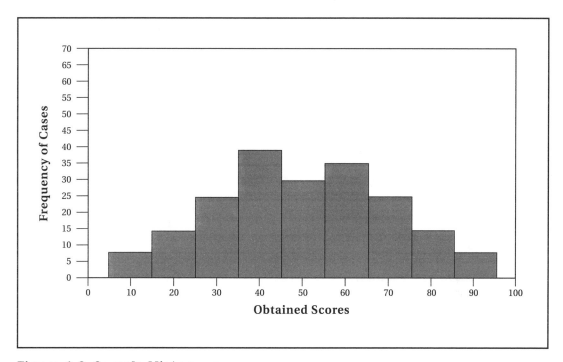

Figure 6.2. Sample Histogram

Line Charts

Line charts can be used make comparisons of groups of continuous data. Each line represents a different group while the points on the lines represent the obtained values for each measurement period. The horizontal axis represents a continuous variable, such as time, and the vertical axis represents the frequency data. When constructing the line chart, each line should be distinct from one another and a legend should indicate what each line represents. The horizontal and vertical axes should be labeled and each should have equally spaced divisions along the measurement scales. Titles should be provided for the axes indicating the form of the measurement and the units. Finally, the chart should have a title describing the data represented in the chart. A sample line chart is in Figure 6.3.

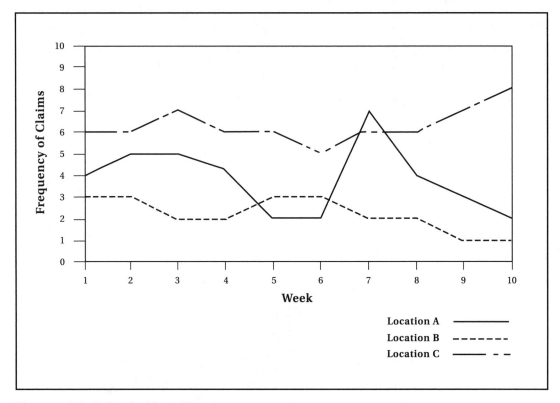

Figure 6.3. Sample Line Chart

Tables

Tables are used to summarize frequency data arranged in rows and columns. Tables are meant to supplement the text, not duplicate it (American Psychological Association 1995, 125). Titles and when necessary, footnotes should be provided with the tables. The title provides a clear meaning as to the information contained within and, if appropriate, the source of the data and the time frame from which the data was obtained. Footnotes may accompany the table to provide additional information about the data and variables. Table 6.1 is an example.

Table 6.1. Summary of Losses by Department: 2002[a]

	Losses ($)	Percent (%)
Production	$20,000	20
Human Resources	$5,000	5
Engineering	$1,000	1
Maintenance	$75,000	74
Total	$101,000	100

[a]Losses are based upon paid insurance claims.

Bar Charts

Bar charts are used to make visual comparisons between two or more categorical variables that have been measured along a continuum. For example, the number of injuries by body part can be compared across departments using a bar chart. To construct a bar chart, each category of data for which comparisons are to be made (in this example the department in which the injury occurred) are represented by different colored or shaded bars. Thus all of the bars from one department are the same color or shade and can be readily distinguishable from the bars representing other departments. The category for which the data was subdivided, in this example, the type of injury by body part, is identified along the horizontal axis. Separating the categories allows for a comparison between type of injury as well as type of injury by department.

In this example, the vertical axis represents the frequency of cases. An equal area of the bar then represents each case. Therefore, a bar representing 20 cases would be two times higher than a bar that represents 10 cases. Additional features of a bar chart include a title indicating the source of the data and a legend that identifies the meaning of the bars. An example of a bar chart appears in Figure 6.4.

Pie Charts

Pie charts provide a graphic representation of data in which the data comprises 100 percent of the sample or population. The wedges of the pie represent the subdivisions of the data, with each slice labeled as to the category it represents and the percentage for which it accounts. When ordering the slices of pie in the chart, the segments should be ordered from largest to smallest beginning with the largest segment at 12:00 (American Psychological Association 1995, 143). Figure 6.5 is an example.

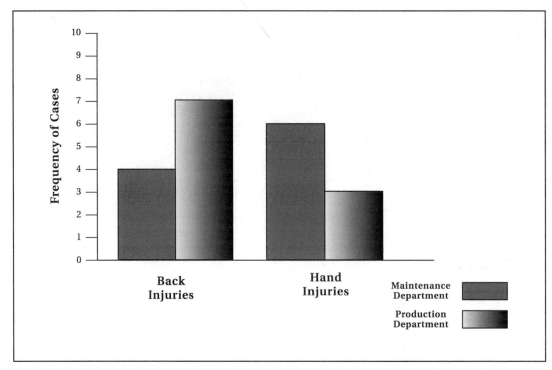

Figure 6.4. Sample Bar Chart

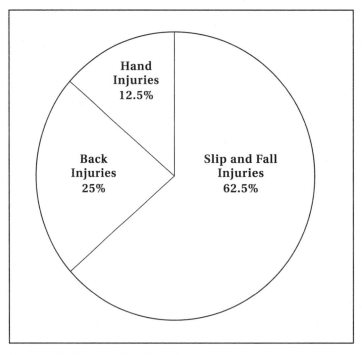

Figure 6.5. Sample Pie Chart

Summary

An important part of improving safety performance is the ability for the safety professional to effectively communicate to management and employees. Because safety
performance can be heavily weighted in quantitative measures, the safety manager
should be able to properly display data and the results of analyses so that the information is conveyed clearly. Some of the more common techniques for displaying
performance measure data includes the use of tables, line graphs, bar charts, and pie
charts. Statistical information about the findings related to the population can also
be conveyed through the use of histograms.

Chapter Questions

1. What is a scatterplot used to represent?
2. What is the difference between the variable plotted along the horizontal axis versus the vertical axis on a scatterplot?
3. The following data was collected from Company CJD. Develop a histogram that
   represents the data:

Subject	Measurement
1	50
2	51
3	50
4	49
5	48
6	50
7	51
8	50
9	49
10	50
11	51
12	48
13	50
14	50
15	51
16	50
17	49
18	50
19	51
20	48

4. The following data was collected from Company CJD. Develop a line chart that represents the data:

Time	Group #1	Group #2	Group #3
8:00 a.m.	3	2	2
9:00 a.m.	2	3	3
10:00 a.m.	3	3	3
11:00 a.m.	5	1	1
12:00 p.m.	4	4	4
1:00 p.m.	2	4	4
2:00 p.m.	1	5	5
3:00 p.m.	5	4	4
4:00 p.m.	4	2	2
5:00 p.m.	5	2	2

5. The following data was collected from Company CJD. Develop a pie chart that represents the data:

	Hand Injuries	Back Injuries	Leg Injuries
Number of Cases	13	36	4

6. The following data was collected from Company CJD. Develop a table that represents the data:

Group	Production	Quality Assurance	Maintenance
	Male	Male	Male
	Female	Female	Female
	Male	Male	Male
	Female	Male	Male
	Male	Male	Male
	Female	Male	Female
	Male	Female	Male
	Female	Male	Male
	Male	Male	Male
	Male	Male	Female

7. What type of data are bar charts typically used to represent?
8. What type of data are line charts typically used to represent?
9. When developing a table to present data, what are some general guidelines for developing the table?
10. When developing a line chart to present data, what are some general guidelines for developing the chart?

Establishing a Safety Metrics Program

A safety metrics program requires the same managerial support and organization as any other type of activity in the workplace. Like these other workplace activities, a key component of the metrics program includes a structured management system necessary for the development and implementation of the program. The management system should establish the program leadership and methods for establishing accountability. Implementing the program involves identifying safety measurement needs, developing program objectives and the processes for implementing the program, determining corrective action, and ensuring follow up.

Leadership

Developing effective leadership can provide the following benefits (Simmons 1997, 273):

- managers at all levels providing a more strategic approach to planning improvements
- managers increasing their ability to overcome resistance and encourage the whole-hearted involvement of people in continual improvement activities
- employees contributing their energy and commitment more willingly to the aims of the organization
- individuals improving their performance when working in teams and project groups
- better relationships between customers, suppliers, and people in other departments

Effective leaders have understood that their job is to lead a process of systematic organizational transformation. To be fully effective, this process of organizational transformation, must tackle three areas (Simmons 1997, 273):

(1) Managing the future in a turbulent environment: This situation cannot be resolved without management involving people at every level of the enterprise in planning how to manage the future. People need to understand and 'appreciate' what is happening, feel a part of a process for managing it, and share a unifying sense of direction to guide them through the uncertainty. Creating opportunities for

everyone to align their personal goals with the organization's goals, and then planning together how to get there has become an essential component of effective transformation.

(2) Improving productivity and quality: This has become a priority for any enterprise wishing to survive in the world of international competition. People, as customers, are exercising increasing judgment about the products and services they buy and receive, and they will only favor those that reach the very highest standards. Moreover, every corporation throughout the world is looking systematically at how to produce 'more for less', and, therefore, finding ways to improve productivity is a necessity for everyone.

(3) Building an 'inclusive organization': The most important asset remaining untapped in many organizations is the huge reservoir of ability in its people. They must begin to build an 'inclusive organization', which is one which reaches systematically to ensure that everyone is included, that everyone's contribution is valued and that difference is embraced as an asset rather than a limitation.

In pursuing these goals, leaders will focus their organization on three key activities (Simmons 1997, 274):

(1) enabling everyone in the enterprise to develop a shared vision of the future and planning how to achieve it

(2) developing a culture of innovation and continual improvement towards all products and processes

(3) taking positive action to enable everyone, at all levels, to contribute their full potential towards the vision and their own work

Accountability

Accountability consists of four parts: people, time, milestones, and formality (Pierce 1995, 127). To make someone or a group accountable for a task or responsibility, one must first identify that person or team. Second, one must set an agreed upon a time or date for task completion. Third, if the task will take a long time, is complex, or the person or team is on a learning curve, milestones should be set—times or dates along the path toward completion where progress is tracked. Finally, and very importantly, there must be a formal system, including a written objective, a person charged with the objective, and written targeted completion dates and milestones.

In an effective safety and health program, everything is formal and interwoven together: vision, mission, planning, goals, objectives, accountability, participation, training, communication, and rewards (Pierce 1995, 127). There must be a tie-in to the performance management system because without a reward system, accountability is tough to maintain. The safety performance program must be tied to the performance management system the organization uses to measure and reward employees by their pay.

Collaborative Process

The development of performance measures requires a collaborative effort from various levels of the organization, as well as personnel from different departments, such as safety, environmental, finance, personnel, maintenance, and engineering. The inputs the various departments can provide include appropriate benchmark levels, validity of performance measures, data needs (such as methods for obtaining data, available data, and data collection means), audit procedures, and evaluation techniques. Input from the various departments can be useful in determining available sources so that duplication does not result in wasted time and money.

Collaboration does not have to end with personnel and departments within an organization. When establishing performance measures, techniques used by other facilities within the company or industry can lend valuable insight into methods already in use. These techniques may be available from the companies or from professional organizations. The positive results from a collaborative effort include minimal duplication of work and a broader perspective of what should be measured as well as the steps involved in collecting and analyzing the information.

Defining Organizational Processes

A thorough understanding of the organization and its processes is necessary in order to develop meaningful objectives and goals. These processes should be defined in operational terms and these terms should be used in the objectives and goals. Use a collaborative, team approach to define a process. Team members with diverse organizational responsibilities can provide a more objective outcome and precisely defined process. Flowcharting should be used to indicate key components of the process and their respective roles. (The process flow chart is the primary tool for analyzing the process to determine whether there are deficiencies [Juran and Godfrey 1999, 411]). Without a properly defined process, difficulty arises when trying to assess performance in the safety metrics program.

Measurement

For each of the components of the program to function properly, the proper data must be identified and collected. Valid and reliable data are the foundation for an effective metrics program. Data necessary to measure safety performance must be identified, attainable, and relate back to the overall program goals and objectives. "One of the areas most often forgotten or misapplied in managing goals and objectives is measurement" (Pierce 1995, 129).

For the safety performance to improve in the workplace, interventions must be based upon sound information that begins with the measurement process. Proper measurement and collection of safety metrics requires employees to be motivated to keep abreast as to where the safety program stands with regard to the goals that have been set. Employees in the organization should be held accountable for collecting the necessary measurements for the metrics program. Measurement activities should be established to ensure validity and reliability of the data. Inconsistencies in the measurement will lead to invalid data, improper conclusions, and incorrect corrective action.

Resources and Documentation

In order to develop and maintain a safety metrics program, various resources must be identified. These resources include data sources and measurement techniques. If a more traditional approach to measuring safety performance is utilized, such as accident and injury rates, the data should be available and if not, part of the metrics program should involve the procedures for collecting the data and collating it at a central location for analysis.

Documentation may include the procedures for the collection, analysis, and compilation of the measurements. Benchmarks, the comparisons of the measurements to the benchmarks, and the follow-up required by those results, should be included in the documentation. Additional resources may include financial and personnel resources needed to make the program work. Complex measurement and analysis programs may run into problems if adequate personnel and financial resources are not made available.

Documentation requirements can include the procedures developed to implement the program, training program goals, safety standards, and blueprints and diagram for processes used in a facility. In the initial stages of the program development, an accounting of necessary documentation should be addressed.

Data Collection

When developing the objectives for the safety performance program established, the data needs should be identified. Data concerns that should addressed early involve determining if the data needed for the performance measures exist and if so, is the data reliable and readily available. Also, in order to measure a safety performance objective effectively, more than one measure may be needed. It is best to use a variety of measures to ascertain performance rather than just one. Multiple measures provide a better picture of the true status of the safety performance.

The data as discussed earlier should also have the characteristics of being valid and reliable. To be considered valid, the data has been tested and found to measure what it is intended to measure. For the data to be considered a reliable measure, the data reflect consistency in the measures.

Procedures for the collection of the data should be developed and documented. Pertinent information as to how the data is recorded, when it is documented, and the frequency at which the data is collected is an important aspect of the data collection process. A procedure that infuses consistency over time in the data collection process will generate better comparisons, thus allowing the safety manager to draw more meaningful conclusions.

There are a variety of data collection systems available to the safety manger in the workplace. Some of these data collection systems include direct measurement, indirect measurement, statistical samples, and interviews (Czarnecki 1999):

1. Direct measurement systems are usually used when there is a unit of production or an event that is captured in an automated system such as a computer. The count is very reliable because it counts events that are actually happening.

2. Indirect measurement systems are used when the actual data is not collected at the time the event occurs. This indirect method is usually not as good as the direct method because it depends heavily on the accuracy of the alternate data source.

3. Statistical samples can be used to develop estimates where whole data is incomplete. In the event that there are a large number of transactions for which there are no summaries, it may be necessary to perform statistical sampling to determine an approximate measure.

4. Interviews or surveys to gather metric information are used as a last resort. Some companies have resorted to face-to-face interviews to determine measurements when other sources were unavailable. Interviews are most helpful when the measures are perceptual, but keep in mind that perceptual measures contain inherent imprecision and bias.

Coordinating Measures

General guidelines for identifying data needs and developing the data collection tools can be developed depending upon if the data required to support the measurement already exists (Training Resources and Data Exchange [TRADE] 1995, 1-19). If data to support the performance measure already exists, then the development of the data collection system consists of documenting the data source, defining the procedures for retrieving the data, and reviewing the data for potential inconsistencies. If additional data needs are identified, then they should be addressed.

If data to support the performance measure does not exist, then a process of defining the data required as well as creating a consistent and verifiable system to input and store data should be addressed. Accountability for this new data source should be addressed by identifying the person responsible for collecting the data, and defining processes for the collection and processing should be thorough and documented.

Summary

Safety performance programs require the same level of planning and resources as other management programs. Critical characteristics of an effective safety performance program include leadership, accountability, and collaboration. A team approach to safety performance and the safety program is necessary for any program to function. Resource needs, documentation, and data requirements should be addressed early in the planning stages of the program.

Chapter Questions

1. Provide three examples of benefits that effective leadership can provide a safety metrics program.
2. Describe three activities leaders should focus an organization on.
3. Describe the four parts of accountability.
4. Define collaboration.
5. What are the basic requirements of the data used in a performance program?
6. Provide some examples of resources that can be used to collect information pertaining to safety performance.
7. Describe some major downfalls to a safety performance program with regards to data.
8. Characteristics of ideal data that can be used in a safety performance program include:
9. Describe four different types of measurement systems.
10. Describe the overall framework for a safety metrics program.

8

Benchmarking

Benchmarking is an ongoing process of measuring one company's safety performance against that of competitors or organizations that are recognized as industry leaders. The benchmarking process requires an organization to identify other organizations that are considered best in their field, identify what makes the others the best, then work to attain that same level through a continual improvement process. In other words, benchmarking is simply learning what other programs and organizations are doing to be successful and using some of those successes in one's own program or organization (Pierce 1995, 176).

Benchmarking serves as a measuring stick for the organization by identifying those organizations that are viewed as the best. Benchmarking can also be used to identify areas of weakness and assist in prioritizing program improvements. Finally, benchmarking provides a mechanism for continuous improvement. It serves as a standard toward achieving and maintaining excellence in the program or organization (Pierce 1995, 179).

When benchmarking safety performance, the safety manager identifies the organizations that can be considered the leaders in terms of various safety performances. One should keep in mind that while one organization can be considered the best in terms of lost workday cases, another company can be considered the best in another aspect of the safety program. The overall purpose and intent of benchmarking can be summarized as the (Holloway, Lewis, and Mallory 1995, 128):

- Development of an understanding of the fundamentals that create business success, based on an objective measurement of relative performance (both real and perceived) against relevant companies, in areas involving critical business processes.

- Focus on continuous improvement efforts, based on an ongoing analysis of the essential differences between similar processes in comparable businesses, and of the underlying reasons for these differences.

- Management of the overall change process and of the individual changes involved in achieving the improvements, based on the development and implementation of action programs to close the gap between a company and the 'best-in-class' companies with the most relevant key performance variables.

Benchmarking can readily be applied to the safety function in an organization. A structured approach should be followed for selecting measures for which the benchmarks are based. Examples of benchmarks in safety include outcomes-based measures such as accident rates and losses and performance-based measures such as the implementation of a hazard recognition program or employee training programs. Prior to making changes in the workplace, the safety manager must carefully select the proper performance measures that are indicative of the benchmarks established. For example, a safety manager has been experiencing a high frequency of back injuries in the facility and decides to establish a benchmark for the company for this area of the safety program performance. The safety manager obtains accident data from a variety of other organizations related to their back injury experience and information pertaining to the accident prevention activities that the companies engage in to control back injuries in the workplace. To effectively reach the benchmarks, the safety manager must decide if the activities the other organizations are engaged in are adequate or if there are other activities that should be implemented that are unique to the company (e.g., material handling hazards). The safety manager must then develop performance measures for activities in order to determine if they help to reach the benchmarks.

Defining Safety Benchmarks

Benchmarking can be undertaken in almost any area of business and organizational endeavor, including safety performance. The basic requirement is that key performance variables are identified, measured, analyzed, and compared to provide a basis for planned performance improvement. An optimum benchmark can be characterized by the following (Holloway, Lewis, and Mallory 1995, 134):

1. The benchmark should be measurable in terms of cost, time, value, or some other quantitative parameter.
2. The benchmark should be meaningful and relevant.
3. Benchmarks that use simple performance measures are often the best and the most easily accessible.
4. The benchmarks should be available in external and competitive environments.
5. If an actual external measure cannot be obtained, a well-founded estimate should be used as a substitute.

In many companies, such safety performance variables are found internally through accident reporting and safety recordkeeping. The safety manager needs to identify those measures that are key to safety performance success. The key is to be clear about the needs and what it is important to improve. Overall, there are four different types of benchmarking that a safety manager can use: internal, functional, competitive, and generic (Holloway, Lewis, and Mallory 1995, 129–30).

Internal benchmarking is done within an organization and typically between closely related divisions, similar plants or operations, or equivalent business units, using common or shared performance parameters as a basis for comparison. Because of the relative ease of starting a new activity internally, the lower resource implications, and the higher assurance of gaining cooperation, this is the area in which many organizations choose to start benchmarking activities. This is valuable in gaining initial knowledge, experience and commitment, but is limited to internal criteria only. Examples of internal benchmarks for safety include accident data and activity measures such as training programs completed and hazard surveys conducted.

Functional benchmarking is a comparison of performance and procedures between similar business functions, but in different organizations and industries. It represents a more positive approach than internal benchmarking by being externally focused. However, in relating only to specific functions, it may not be of wider benefit in other areas of the organizations concerned. Functional benchmarks for safety could involve making comparisons to different organizations and industries in terms of lost work days, recordable injuries, and workers' compensation losses.

Competitive benchmarking generally focuses on direct competitors within the same industry and with specific comparable business operations, or on indirect competitors in related industries (perhaps key customers or suppliers) having complementary business operations. There are often practical difficulties with sourcing information, and activities may be limited to arm's-length comparisons.

Generic benchmarking is undertaken with external companies in different industries, which represent the 'best-in-class' for particular aspects of the selected safety measures.

Benchmarking Process

The benchmarking process involves comparing a company's safety experiences with other companies and organizations. Organizations use the performance results from others to define their benchmarks and strive to meet those levels. Best practices in benchmarking can be set, at each stage, by posing four fundamental performance questions (Holloway, Lewis, and Mallory 1995, 129):

- Are we performing better than we ever have?
- Are we performing better than other plants or business units in the company?
- Are we performing better than our competitors?
- Are there any other industries that are performing well and from whom we can learn?

Benchmarking can be defined as a six-part process. They are surveying, identification, prioritization, developing a plan, implementing a plan, and follow-up (Pierce

1995, 177–78). These steps in the benchmarking process are described in detail in the following sections.

Surveying: The first part in benchmarking is surveying "front running" programs or organizations. There is a critical need to identify the programs or organizations that are truly front running. Once front-running organizations or programs are selected, the sites are visited or telephoned to see how they operate. A survey is used to gather information and determine how other safety programs operate.

Identification: The second part of benchmarking is identifying the complementary solutions used by the target organization or program. The solutions are only "complementary" because the purpose of benchmarking is not to build a replica of the target.

Prioritization: Part three of benchmarking is prioritizing the "growth opportunities" from the list of complementary solutions. This step involves determining where the safety program weaknesses exist.

Develop a Plan: Develop a plan to achieve growth. The plan can be used to identify the areas to pursue.

Implementing the plan: This step involves the implementation of the plan that has been developed.

Follow-up: Benchmarking is a dynamic process. Once the plan has been implemented, the next step is the ongoing aspect of the process, the follow-up. At regular, scheduled intervals, resurvey, reprioritize, refine the plan, and redirect the implementation.

Motorola Corporation has developed its five-step benchmarking plan. This plan consists of the following steps (Hodgetts 1998, 196):

1. The topics that are to be benchmarked are identified.

2. The approach to be used for gathering data is determined.

3. Benchmarking partners who are the best in terms of the functions and processes being studied are identified, and a partnering agreement is formulated for the mutual exchange of information.

4. The benchmarking partner's approach is carefully studied in order to answer two questions: What enables them to be the best? How do they do it?

5. An action plan is created for both analyzing the data and implementing follow-up action.

Continuous Improvement Process

Benchmarking uses total quality management principles to integrate safety management techniques, existing improvement efforts and technical tools into a disciplined approach focused on continuous improvement. Continuous improvement is essential in increasing safety performance and alleviating waste of employee time and company resources (Kaufman, Thiagarajan, and Sivasailam 1997).

An underlying premise of continuous improvement process can be depicted in terms of the classic plan-do-check-act (PDCA) management cycle. This PDCA cycle can also be found as a management strategy in various ISO standards, including ISO 9000. With this strategy, the following steps are implemented as a means for meeting this continuous improvement (Juran and Godfrey 1999, 41.3–41.4):

- **Plan** objectives for quality safety and the methods to achieve them
- **Do** the appropriate resource allocation, training, and documentation
- **Check** to see if the things have been implemented as planned, objectives are being met, and the objectives set are relevant to program needs
- **Act** to improve the system as needed

Benchmarking Pitfalls

Some of the major pitfalls identified with benchmarking include the costs associated with its implementation, the lack of predictive power, the potential difficulty in obtaining information for which to benchmark against, and a significant lag time between implementation and results.

Compared with other types of analysis techniques, benchmarking does not have any predictive power to anticipate future performance, results, or benefits (Holloway, Lewis and Mallory 1995, 148). Although great care may have been taken in the analysis of other companies and the activities they developed to reach certain performance levels, there is no guarantee that those same activities will yield the same results in another organization. The differences may be due to a number of reasons, including a perceived cause and effect between performance and the activities that really does not exist, differences in the organizations' safety climates, and differences in the exposure levels to various hazards in the workplace.

Costs have also been identified as a potential problem with benchmarking. When done properly, the benchmarking process requires a substantial amount of time and resources analyzing other companies' data and activities, developing and implementing new activities in the workplace, and the ongoing continual improvement process of data collection, analysis, and modifications.

A third area that can become a problem for benchmarking is the availability of valid data from other organizations. In order to establish effective benchmarks, one must know the performance levels of other organizations. It may be difficult to obtain the necessary data from other companies, and if it is obtained, comparisons may be difficult due to differences in measurements used across industries.

Fourth, the benchmarking process requires a considerable amount of time from when the decision is made to benchmark to when measurable results are realized. As with any safety program activity designed to improve performance, the results of the performance may not be evident for some time. In the case of measuring activities designed to increase the workers' use of personal protective equipment, results may be evident in a relatively short period of time following the implementation of the program. Supervisors can go out to the production areas and observe worker performance. However, in the case where the activity is supposed to reduce the number of recordable injuries, the lag time may be a year before the decrease in cases can be substantiated.

Summary

For safety performance to improve, the safety manager must establish goals. Benchmarking is the process through which the organization identifies the best safety performing companies and strives to meet or exceed their performance levels. Continual improvement is the process through which benchmarking can be used to improve performance. While it can be a time and resource-consuming process, benchmarking is a successful and worthwhile endeavor for a variety of organizations.

Chapter Questions

1. Define the term "benchmarking."
2. What functions does benchmarking serve for an organization?
3. An optimum benchmark can be characterized by what qualities?
4. Differentiate between internal benchmarking, functional benchmarking, competitive benchmarking, and generic benchmarking.
5. Describe the six steps in the benchmarking process.
6. Describe the "continuous improvement process."
7. Describe the PDCA management cycle.
8. Describe some disadvantages to benchmarking.
9. Describe the five-step benchmarking process used by Motorola Corporation.

Auditing Safety Performance

In order to monitor the success of a safety program, both a successful auditing program and quality safety metrics are needed because audits are another technique used in the evaluation and data collection process of the program. An audit or inspection is the monitoring function conducted in an industrial organization to locate and report existing and potential hazards, or man-environment systems or conditions, that have the capacity to cause accidents or illnesses in the workplace (Petersen 1998).

The audit process in a safety program helps improve a firm's overall safety performance by identifying and eliminating potential hazards. As part of the safety performance improvement process, safety audits are a method of obtaining data with regards to the current status of the safety program. Information obtained from safety audits include the extent to which hazards are present, the identification of newly discovered problems that may affect the organization's ability to meet performance objectives, and conformation of work practices and their relationship to the organization's procedures. Data obtained from the safety audits can then be used to quantify current performance and determine if the safety performance is meeting the desired goals and benchmarks. As is the case for other methods designed to measure performance in the workplace, safety audits must also possess the characteristics of validity and reliability.

Compliance of the safety process to laws, regulations, and company policies and procedures is measured effectively by audits. Self-audits can be effective, if done with objective honesty. More than 85 percent of employers in a recent Occupational Safety and Health Administration survey said they conduct voluntary self-audits of safety and health conditions in their workplaces (IIE Solutions 1999, 12). With a 60% increase over an 18-year period in the number of organizations indicating they conduct audits, nearly 90 percent of the respondents indicated they had conducted an audit in the past 12 months (IIE Solutions 1999, 12). Reasons for conducting these audits include the need to reduce accidents, to do what is considered right for worker safety and health, and to ensure OSHA compliance. Additional motivators for organizations to conduct audits include decreases in injury rates, improvement in insurance rates, and mitigating fines from OSHA violations.

Types of Audits

Audits can be classified a number of ways. One method of classifying audits is by the relationship of the auditor to the organization. If the auditor is from within the organization, the audit is considered internal. If the auditor if from outside the organization, the audit can be considered external. Internal audits are any organization-initiated hazard survey, inspection, or job observation. The criteria for the audits, audit process, and use of the information all begin within the organizational structure. External audits are initiated and performed from outside the organization. Examples of external audits include OSHA inspections, insurance company inspections, and any other jurisdictions that may have the authority to inspect a company. Regardless of the type of inspection, both provide valuable information to the organization and both can be used in the performance evaluation of the company. In some situations, the external audits may be weighted more heavily in terms of safety performance measure partly because of the potential impact the findings may have on an organization (i.e., fines and violations) and because the auditors may be considered more objective since they are external to the company.

The second method for classifying audits is in terms of their frequency of conducting them. Additional classes of audits are planned, unplanned, and continuous (Daugherty 1999, 137). Planned audits occur periodically in the organization on a schedule that is known to the company. Unplanned audits occur with no prior announcement to the organization. Planned and unplanned audits serve different purposes. Planned audits serve to guide a program's development and determine how activities are functioning and being implemented. Unplanned audits are most commonly used in the enforcement of safety and health regulations. Unplanned audits are used to determine if the company is doing what is expected of them at all times.

Audit Personnel

Management has the ultimate responsibility for auditing, but should get as many people involved as practical in the auditing process. Foremen, supervisors, safely committee members, safety engineers, and plant managers are all potential inspectors.

To ensure the audit process produces valid and reliable information, several aspects of an audit program should be developed. The audit process may require the auditor to make judgment calls with regards to the status of a work condition. To provide some degree of consistency in the conclusions reached about a situation among auditors, auditing procedures, scoring criteria, and auditor training and practice should be part of the audit program. Auditing procedures can aid in data quality improvement by establishing guidelines pertaining to the items that are addressed in an audit and the frequency of audits. Scoring criteria should be established to improve the reliability of the audit instrument. A hazard identified by one auditor should receive the same score when found by another auditor. Auditor training and practice will also be beneficial in improving consistency among auditors.

Constructing Audits

The manner in which the audit instrument is constructed will obviously have a significant impact upon the audit program and the results. The instrument must be designed in a manner that will solicit valid and reliable results. The validity of the instrument is an indication of how well the instrument is measuring what it is supposed to be measuring. For example, if an audit instrument is intended to measure the organization's compliance with fire protection requirements, then the instrument should be evaluating those areas of the organization that are indicative of fire protection compliance.

Another key characteristic of the audit instrument is that of reliability. If an instrument is reliable, it should provide the same results when administered multiple times at the same time. A key factor that can influence the reliability of the audit instrument is the auditor completing the instrument. If two auditors using the same instrument and the same time complete an audit, one would expect to obtain the same findings. Factors that influence how one auditor may obtain results that are different from another in this situation include the wording of the audit items, the instructions provided, and the auditor training and understanding of the audit process.

Companies can define the scope and focus of the audit in terms of organizational, geographical, functional, and compliance contexts (National Safety Council 1997, 102). These boundaries include departments within the organization, activities, and safety areas such as fire protection, industrial hygiene, and machine guarding. The audit instrument should provide the auditor with a thorough understanding of the scope of the audit process. This would ensure that areas that need to be addressed are not bypassed. The audit protocol is the auditor's plan to accomplish the objectives of the audit (National Safety Council 1997, 107). The protocol provides the auditor with instructions on the locations to audit and the areas that should be addressed. Descriptions of the situations that indicate compliance and non-compliance with the audit protocol should be included with the audit items.

Linking Audits to Performance Measures

A key characteristic of an audit that is seldom examined is the link between audit performance and safety performance in the workplace. For example, if the objective of an audit is to evaluate accident prevention strategies in the workplace, then there should be some type of correlation or relationship between performance in the audit and accident history. All too often, audits are developed and items appear on them because they should be a part of the safety program, when in actuality some activities that are commonly part of a safety program may not have any relationship with accident involvement. Suppose a company meets all of the requirements of the audit over a period of time and the safety performance worsens. This does not mean that the safety activities are increasing accident rates. More likely, it means that the items being evaluated through the audit are not influencing accident prevention. Incorrect linking of audits to accident and safety performance sends management the wrong information. The audits may indicate that safety program is working when it really may not be, or areas of the safety program that appear on the audit may be working but may not be measured by the safety performance metrics.

The objective in making and using an effective audit tool for the purpose of measuring safety performance is to determine the correlation between the audit, its individual items, and the safety performance measure.

Audit instruments can be evaluated on the basis of three different types of validity when linking the audit to safety performance. These are content-related, criterion-related, and construct-related procedures for accumulating evidence of validity (Anastasi 1988, 139). Content-related validity involves the examination of the audit content to determine whether it covers a representative sample of the behaviors to be measured. Criterion-related validity procedures indicate the effectiveness of an audit in predicting performance in specified activities. The performance on the audit is checked against a criterion that is considered a direct and independent measure of what the audit was intended to measure. The third type of validity, construct validity, is the extent to which the audit is said to be measuring a theoretical construct or trait. Construct validation requires accumulation of information from a variety of sources.

The Audit Process

The audit process consists of collecting information about the physical conditions of the workplace as well as the safety performance. The most important aspect of the audit process is the action that is implemented following the audit. If the results from the audit indicate that performance is below expectations, then action needs to be taken. All too often, the audit process ends at the collection of the information with no further action, thus making the audit process useless.

A follow-up or deficiency tracking system should be devised so that appropriate personnel may be held accountable. Assign a tracking number to each deficiency and record the date, location, and a brief description of the finding. What is the appropriate OSHA standard for corrective measures? Record its hazard rating by potential consequence and probability. List the corrective action required, step-by-step. What is the estimated cost of correction? When was it corrected? How much did it actually cost to correct?

Once the audits have been completed, it is equally important to disseminate the results of the audit findings to the organization. Again, to make the audit program effective as possible, those that may need to take action or monitor the safety performance in the organization need to know the results of the audit process.

A third important component of the audit process is the performance indexing of the audit results. The task of performance indexing requires the results of the audit to be quantified in a manner that allows for comparisons against performance benchmarks. While the actual audits may identify the number of unsafe actions performed by personnel during an observation period, the raw numbers are really meaningless until they are placed in a context which is comparable to an established index. The performance indices established from an audit can include the percentages of unsafe acts performed, the frequencies of hazardous conditions identified, or the accident rates for a period of time to name a few.

In summary, successful auditing programs begin with a structured process of collecting data by qualified personnel. The data collected from the audits must be organized in a manner that will allow personnel to make judgments about the status of the safety program and make comparisons against established acceptable levels of performance. Finally, the most important aspect of the audit program is the follow up. The purpose of the program is a mechanism for improvement; therefore, the decisions made and corrective actions following the audit will ultimately determine the success of the program.

Potential Problems with Audits

While audits and the audit process can be a very effective tool for collecting information and evaluating safety performance, they can also pose some potential problems for an organization. Some examples of potential problems with audits include (Daugherty 1999, 136):

1. Can be construed as faultfinding
2. May produce only a superficial laundry list
3. May produce no remedial actions
4. May produce only inadequate remedial action

Audit programs require the same key elements as any other safety program activity. These four elements include top management commitment, a humanistic approach towards employees, one-on-one contact, and the use of positive reinforcement (Petersen 1998). Studies however, have found that most safety audit programs have top management commitment but are lacking in the other three areas (Petersen 1998). If lacking in these areas, the safety audit program may not meet the needs for which it is intended. The shortcomings include missing problems areas where they do exist and focusing on areas where problems do not exist (Emery and Savely 1997, 39). As a result, audit programs may be failing to provide sufficient feedback for program improvement.

Benefits of Audits

Audits and the auditing program provide a variety of benefits to the safety program. Some direct benefits of an audit program include:

- They provide data for the purpose of evaluating the safety performance in a company.
- They provide the safety manager with an indication as to the current status of activities in the workplace.
- When properly implemented, they serve as an objective means for evaluating the safety program against established benchmarks.

Some indirect benefits of the audit program include:

- The auditing program communicates management's commitment to safety.
- The audit program provides a means for employee involvement in terms of the actual conduct of the audit and in terms of allowing employee input during the audit process.

Summary

Auditing is one process a safety manager can use to collect data for the safety improvement program. The audit process has been used extensively in the safety field for years; however, some research has suggested safety managers should carefully scrutinize the development and implementation of a new program. Rather than going through the facility with a checklist, marking off items and filling in the sheet, a safety manager should realize the importance of the role the audit process fills in collecting data for measuring performance.

Chapter Questions

1. Describe the purpose of the auditing process in a safety performance measurement program.
2. Describe three areas that audits can be used to obtain data for a safety metrics program.
3. Describe three purposes an audit can serve for an organization.
4. Differentiate between a planned audit and a continuous. What are some examples of each.
5. For an audit program, describe some personnel factors one should address when implementing such a program.
6. Describe some characteristics a good audit instrument should follow.

7. Differentiate between the validity of an audit instrument and its reliability.

8. Describe some problems that can arise if the audit is not properly linked to the organization's performance.

9. Describe the importance that follow-up action has in the audit process.

10. What are some benefits and problems with audits and the audit process?

Insurance Rating Systems

Many organizations view safety not only as a method for protecting people's lives and property but also as a means for achieving and maintaining financial objectives. There are a number of safety metrics that can be used to evaluate and monitor the financial impact that the safety program is having upon the company. While counting accidents and injuries is a common method of evaluating the protection of employees, financial accounting of losses and insurance costs are valid methods for measuring the safety performance in terms of financial performance. Using financial measures of insurance losses, claims, and expenses is also a common method of quantifying safety performance. These measures can be tracked over time and as safety and loss control efforts are directed toward these losses, an indication of their effectiveness can be ascertained.

Insurance Terms

Before it is possible to begin using insurance expenses, losses, and costs as measurements of safety performance, a clear understanding is needed as to what the terms used in the insurance industry mean. Some of the more common terms used in the insurance industry and loss control include the following (Rupp 1991):

Experience rating modification factor: The experience rating modification factor attempts to reflect an insured's actual losses in relation to the same insured's premium. A factor is a number applied to the manual premium to either increase or decrease the insured's final premium. A retrospective plan modifies the premium after the policy period or after most of the policy period, while a prospective plan examines prior periods, such as the last three years, to produce a premium.

Interstate Experience Rating: A multi-state experience rating program developed by the National Council on Compensation Insurance for employers with multi-state operations. The experience of all the states is combined to determine the employer's experience modification.

Manual Premium: The premium developed by multiplying a published workers' compensation employee classification rate by each $100 of payroll for that employee classification.

Modified Premium: The manual premium developed for an employer multiplied by the employer's experience modification.

Loss Ratio: The loss ratio is a formula used by insurers to relate loss expenses to income. Formula: (incurred losses + loss adjustment expenses) ÷ earned premiums.

Expected loss ratio: A formula used by insurance companies to relate expected income to expected losses. The formula for the expected loss ratio is (expected incurred losses + expected loss adjusting expense) ÷ expected earned premiums.

Experience Modification Rate

Common measures for a safety program's performance are insurance expenses and losses. A cost that is often tracked by safety professionals is the organization's worker compensation premiums. Workers' compensation premiums can be calculated in a number of different ways. However, regardless of the method for determining premiums, they provide an excellent indicator for safety performance in the workplace.

One such method for determining workers' compensation premiums is through the use of the experience modification rating (EMR). The EMR is determined by the National Council on Compensation Insurance (NCCI) or other insurance rating groups. The EMR system rates companies based upon the type of work they are engaged in and their past loss history. Using actuary science, the insurer estimates what a firm's losses should have been over a period of time and compares them to their actual losses (Adams 1997, 33).

The EMR is considered an excellent benchmark because it is directly related to operational costs, and it has been normalized for company size, the nature of the operation, and other employer specific factors (Taggart and Carter 1999, 35). The EMR provides the company with an indication as to how their workers' compensation loss performance is over a period of time compared to similar companies. The average losses for an industry are represented by an EMR of 1.00. Companies with EMRs greater than 1.00 are paying a workers' compensation premium that is greater than the industry average, while companies with an EMR less than 1.00 are paying premiums less than the industry average.

Elements of the EMR Formula

There are a number of reasons why the EMR for a company can be greater than 1.00, including no prior loss history (as is the case with a new company) and a history of a high frequency of claims. A high frequency of claims reported, although not resulting in high dollar losses, may adversely affect the company's EMR and its workers' compensation premium more than a few claims of higher total dollar losses. Although the higher frequency claims may have resulted in fewer dollars lost, the insurance company views these smaller claims as a potential for losses.

An additional factor used to calculate the EMR is the company's payroll. Jobs are classified according to a class code and rates are established. Job classes that are considered more hazardous carry a higher premium than those that are less hazardous do. The class code rates are multiplied against each $100 of payroll for that particular job class (Rouse, p. 27). If for example, the Class Code rate is $50 per every $100 of payroll, the total payroll in a given year for that class code is determined and the base premium amount set. If the EMR is 1.00, the rate stays the same. If the EMR is 1.50, the rate is then increased by 50%.

The last component that can affect the organization's EMR is the claim reserves. When a workers' compensation is submitted, a reserve is opened which holds the anticipated losses for that claim. Although the claim may actually result in fewer dollars actually paid out when the claim is settled, it is the reserve amount that the insurance company uses when calculating the EMR. Therefore, it is advantageous for the company to work with the insurance company when administering claims and closing them out in a timely manner.

Insurance Loss Ratios

Insurance loss ratios are another group of measures closely related to EMR. These ratios include loss ratio, expense ratio, and combined ratio. Insurance loss ratios can be a valid measurement of safety quality. Although not as widely used for benchmarking as OSHA rates and EMR, these ratios are important to understanding insurance, which is a financial motivator in the field of safety. Insurance losses can be defined as the following:

> **Incurred Losses:** Incurred losses include both losses paid out as benefits and administrative costs of processing these claims. The earned premium is that portion of the total charged to cover risk taken by the insurance company.

> **Underwriting Expenses:** Underwriting expenses include costs of writing a policy, sales commissions, salaries, office space, etc. The written premium is that portion of the total premium charged to cover these expenses. Typically, the written premium is about 30 percent of the total; the remaining 70 percent covers claims—both legitimate and fraudulent—made against the insurance company.

Expense Ratios

Expense Ratios for insurance claims can be measured as the expense versus the total dollar loss for the claim (Bok and Shields 2001). The expenses are costs to the insured in excess of the losses. Insurers must pay expenses such as special services like attorneys fees, rental fees, supplies, and taxes all of which form a cost of doing business (Bickelhaupt 1983, 66).

The ratios alone do not show the whole picture, so it is important to view the underlying dollar amounts. An increase in expense ratios does not necessarily indicate an increase in expense dollars (Bok and Shields 2001). An increasing expense ratio could just as easily result from a decrease in net written premiums provided that expenses are not decreasing at a quicker pace (Bok and Shields 2001). The first expense is what it costs to write insurance-expenses incurred or "expense ratio" (Bok and Shields 2001). This category includes employee salaries, agent commissions, overhead costs, company cars and other expenses incurred just to open the doors and provide a service. This amount also includes loss adjustment expenses.

Combined Ratios

The expense ratio plus the loss ratio equals the "combined ratio." Although insurers use several different ratios to calculate costs, the combined loss ratio is the simplest. The nationwide average for the combined ratio is approximately 1.07 on all types of business property-casualty insurance, which includes WC, fire, and related policies. Thus, for every $1 taken in, insurance carriers pay out $1.07 (Taggart and Carter 1999). If a firm's combined ratio (a combination of insurer's expenses and a firm's losses) is below 1.00, it is considered a profitable account. If the ratio is 0.50, it is a very profitable account. This can be used as a bargaining chip with the insurer. However, if the firm's combined ratio exceeds 1.00, this may be a forewarning of cancellation or a rate hike.

Summary

The insurance loss experience for an organization is closely related to its safety performance. An understanding of how insurance premiums are calculated and the type of impact accidents can have upon premiums can provide the safety manager with an additional method for measuring safety performance. Along with measures of lost workdays and recordable accidents, insurance industry measures should also be part of the safety performance measurement and improvement process. Examples of quantifiable insurance markers that are indicative of safety performance are loss ratios, experience modification rates, and expense ratios. These insurance industry measures are yet another type of performance measure available to the safety professional.

Chapter Questions

1. What does an experience modification factor represent?
2. What importance do insurance costs have with respect to a safety metrics program?
3. Describe three categories of insurance expenses that can be monitored?
4. Company A had an EMR of .75 while Company B had an EMR of 2.7. Assuming they are the same industries with like types of employment, what conclusions can be drawn?
5. What is an expense ratio?
6. What importance do combined ratios have?
7. What factors can contribute to raising an organization's EMR?
8. Describe three programs that can be implemented to control an organization's EMR.
9. What is a manual premium?
10. What organization may determine a company's EMR?

Behavior-Based Safety Metrics

Behavior-based safety is a safety performance technique that has increased in popularity over the past years. Behavior-based safety refers to a process designed to reduce the frequency of work-related accidents by monitoring safe behaviors and reducing the frequency of negative or inappropriate employee behaviors. Its key premise: the proximate causes of most occupational accidents are frequently occurring, inappropriate employee behaviors (i.e., not wearing proper protective equipment, circumventing a machine guard) (Krause and Hidley 1990, 11).

Behavior-based safety is the result of work by behavior psychologists over the years. Using the techniques from applied psychology, psychologists used combinations of behavior analysis to study industrial performance. In 1979, Thomas Krause, a psychologist and John Hindley, a psychiatrist, examined methods in which psychology could be applied to off-shore oil drilling companies in an effort to improve safety performance (Krause 2001, 28). With the majority of accidents in the workplace due to unsafe acts, a premise of behavior-based safety approach is that identification and removal of motivators of unsafe behaviors and the reinforcement of safe behaviors should improve safety performance in the workplace.

Behavior-Based Safety Process

The behavior-based safety process consists of identifying critical behaviors, establishing baseline safe behavior levels, and developing a continuous improvement mechanism into the program (Krause and Hindley 1990, 115). All of these steps in the process also require employee participation to ensure program support that is vital to an effective program. Critical behaviors can be identified in a number of ways, including the evaluation of past accident history and input from those knowledgeable about the processes in the organization. Benchmarks for safe behavior, referred to as baseline acceptable levels, are measured in terms of the percentage of the time the safe behaviors are observed. Supervisors who have been trained in the behavior-based safety program audit employees through the use of job observations and collect data with respect to the safe behaviors observed. As with any performance program, a continual improvement process is integrated in to the behavior-based safety program.

Benchmarks are established, behaviors are observed and quantified, comparisons are made to the benchmarks, and improvement activities are implemented.

A noted authority on behavior-based safety, E. Scott Geller, identified seven key principles that should serve as guidelines when developing a BBS process or tool for safety management. They are (Geller 1999, 40):

1. Focus intervention on behavior
2. Look at external factors to understand and improve behavior
3. Direct behavior with activators or events antecedent to the behavior
4. Focus on positive consequences to motivate behavior
5. Apply the scientific method to improve behavioral interventions
6. Use theory to integrate information, not limit possibilities
7. Design interventions with consideration of internal feelings and attitudes

All voluntary behavior starts out as other-directed, in the sense that we follow someone else's direction (Geller 1999, 44). This direction can be in the form of training, procedures, etc. After leaning what to do, behaviors enter a self-directed stage in which the person performs the activity in a manner that will elicit a positive response. The self-directed activity may not always result in the desired behavior. Changing self-directed behaviors is often difficult because the motivators are personal (Geller 1999, 44).

There are three major forms of behavior interventions. They are instructional intervention, supportive intervention, and motivational intervention (Geller 1999, 44). Instructional interventions consist of educational sessions, training exercises, and directive feedback. Supportive interventions focus on the application of positive consequences. Positive reinforcement of wanted behaviors increases the likelihood that the behavior will be performed again. Motivational interventions include positive incentive or rewards for targeted behaviors. Negative motivators often are ineffective because the consequence or penalty seems remote and improbable (Geller 1999, 46).

In the traditional approach to BBS, employees and their behaviors are the primary focus. The goal is to educate employees and institute processes that involve them in behavioral analysis, observation, and correction. Typically, employees develop lists of critical work behaviors, observe peers performing work, report these observations to peers, and help develop appropriate corrective actions.

Individual Behavior and BBS

To change behavior in the workplace, there are a variety of interventions available—including incentives, deterrence, education, and persuasion (Bonnie 1999, 91). Incentives and deterrents have been found to be the two greatest motivators for safe behavior. Incentives, or positive reinforcers, will increase the performance of wanted behaviors. Deterrents, or disincentives, are outcomes meant to discourage intentional wrongdoing. Research has shown that education and persuasion alone rarely result in behavior change (Bonnie 1999, 91).

Objectives of Measuring Safety Performance

The primary objective of measuring safety performance is to provide a feedback mechanism that will foster continuous improvement. A process for implementing such a program relies on the following steps (Krause and Hidley 1990, 161):

Identifying problem areas: The safety mechanism that is geared for performance measurement and feedback takes its cue from the facility inventory of critical behaviors. Problem areas can be defined as those workplace behaviors that deviate from the expected critical behaviors.

Stimulating preventive action: Based upon the problem areas identified, preventive activities can be directed toward those areas, thus focusing management's attention and resources to the areas that need them the most.

Documenting safety efforts: Without accurately documenting safety efforts, there is no true accountability for managers and supervisors. Nor is there a developing record of facility safety performance trends and profiles.

Reinforcing improvements in behavior: The strongest reinforcement for behavior is feedback that is soon, certain, and positive. In order to reinforce improvement, one must know what types of behaviors lead to the improvement.

Critical Behaviors

Critical behaviors are those behaviors that have been identified as being critical to safety performance in the workplace. These behaviors can be identified using one of four different sources: incident reports, employee interviews, job observations, and review of work rules and procedure manuals.

Incident reports should be the first evaluated item when developing the inventory of critical behaviors (Krause 2001). The accident reports provide the basic foundation of behaviors to target. Typically, three to five years of accident data can provide reliable and valid data. The review of the accident reports can lend insight into the types of behaviors that are most often associated with the organizations accidents.

Interviewing employees can lend insight as to the types of problems that they have encountered while performing job tasks. The employees can also provide information about near miss situations, shortcomings of job procedures. Job observations are useful in documenting the procedures that are followed to complete a task. Reviews of work rules are also useful in determining potential problems with the methods for completing a job task. Together these four approaches can provide the safety professional with an inventory of critical behaviors that can most likely result in an accident.

Seven Factors Critical to BBS Success

In studying behavior-based safety practitioners and implementations, seven factors have been identified as critical to the success of behavior-based safety processes. They are (Hidley 1990, 30–35):

1) Use a process blueprint. To succeed, a firm must have a well-developed blueprint for the entire implementation sequence. This requires a well-structured approach that is implemented rigorously.

2) Emphasize communication, buy-in. Buy-in and communication are related to how well the change effort is "marketed" within the organization.

3) Demonstrate leadership (both management and labor). This factor addresses the central importance of leadership's orientation and support for the change process.

4) Ensure team competence. This factor encompasses identification, recruitment and training of the change-effort steering committee and its leader—a group crucial to success.

5) Use action-oriented training. In a successful initiative, personnel are trained for their roles and responsibilities immediately before they are to be performed. Such a mechanism provides newly trained personnel with success and guidance feedback as they assume new roles—a training version of just-in-time delivery.

6) Use data to ensure continuous improvement. A successful change effort continually measures processes and results.

7) Provide technical resources. Technical assistance influences many aspects of the initiative.

Using Behavior-Based Safety Process as a Safety Metric

The behavior-based safety process lends itself well to a safety metrics program. Establishing safety performance goals and objectives based upon the performance of safe behaviors is the first step in the development of a safety metrics program. With safe behavior goals and objectives established, future activities can be monitored, data can be collected, and comparisons can be made between the activities and the desired levels of performance. When gaps are identified between the desired and actual performance levels, it is up to the safety manager to identify the reasons for the difference and make appropriate changes.

The use of unsafe behaviors as a metric provides the safety manager with an additional tool to use for measuring safety program effectiveness. While accidents and losses are after-the-fact metrics, safety performance based upon unsafe behaviors can be considered a proactive before-the-fact activity, which when used with other metrics, can provide the safety manager with an arsenal of safety metrics.

Behavior-based safety can be used in conjunction with other safety metrics and as part of the overall safety performance program. If the majority of accidents in the workplace are linked to an unsafe act or behavior, decreasing the frequency of these unsafe behaviors should result in a decrease of accidents. Using a multi-pronged safety metrics approach, both unsafe behaviors and unsafe conditions are measured, data collected and analyzed, and performance improvement activities introduced. Behavior-based safety provides the framework for developing standards of performance, collecting data through the use of job observations and the implementation of corrective action. With behavior-based safety, corrective action requires reinforcing safe behavior and discouraging unsafe behavior. While the unsafe behaviors are being addressed through behavior-based safety approach, unsafe conditions can be approached though the same continual improvement process, with engineering approaches used as a corrective action.

The first type of behavior-related measures that can be used before the fact, or before an accident occurs, is the percentage of safe behaviors observed for an observation time. The greater the percentage of safe behaviors, the smaller the percentage of unsafe behaviors, and, thus, the fewer chances for an accident. Other types of measures related to the performance of safe behaviors involve a number of activity-based measures. Some of these may include monitoring the number of job tasks evaluated for potential hazards and compliance with various safety regulations, the number of job tasks for which safe job procedures have been established, and the amount of safety training provided to workers.

Summary

Over the past decade, behavior-based safety has become an integral part of many organizations' safety performance programs. While accidents, lost workdays, and recordable injuries are all measures of after-the-fact performance, behavior-based safety takes a proactive approach. The job behaviors displayed by employees are observed, quantified, and analyzed. Through a structured program that involves employees at all levels of the organization, safe work behaviors are reinforced while unsafe work behaviors are deterred. The performance of safe behaviors can easily be incorporated as another safety metric in the overall safety performance program, thus providing the safety manager with yet another way to measure safety performance in the workplace.

Chapter Questions

1. What does the term behavior-based safety mean?
2. Describe the process of behavior-based safety.

3. What are some examples as to what may influence behaviors in the self directed stage.
4. What is the goal of BBS?
5. What is the primary objective of a BBS program?
6. Define "critical behavior."
7. What are some characteristics of a successful BBS program?
8. How would one go about identifying critical behaviors in an organization?
9. What is the strongest reinforcer for a behavior?
10. Differentiate between an incentive and a deterrent.

12

Evaluating Safety Training

Safety training can be considered one of the most important components of any safety program. Safety training is one specific solution to meet a safety or health need caused by lack of appropriate behavioral skills, related knowledge, and/or attitudes (National Safety Council 1997, 520). Safety training is the key to preventing accidents that are caused by unsafe acts in the workplace; therefore, methods to assess whether the training is effective or not must be developed. Using the methods of safety metrics to evaluate and measure the effectiveness of safety training is a vital component of a safety performance program.

Wexley and Latham (1981) defined four levels of training evaluation—student reaction, learning, behavioral criteria, and results criteria. Each measure is used to assess different aspects of the value of an event.

♦ Student reaction reflects receptiveness to the training. Even though a positive response is desirable, a favorable response does not ensure that learning occurred. Student reaction includes a self-assessment where the student is asked how much they think they learned if given a hypothetical test.

♦ Learning measures are more objective and would include empirical assessments such as a pretests and posttests.

♦ Behavioral measures focus on the actual transfer of knowledge gained for the workplace.

♦ Results measures are similar to behavioral measures with the additional assessment of productivity gain.

The assessment of this effectiveness requires the measurement of safety activities and the ability to determine if the training is meeting the expected safety goals and objectives of the organization. As is the case with other safety program components, there are methodologies available that allow the safety professional to measure and evaluate the safety training. This training assessment can be helpful to (National Safety Council 1997, 523):

1. Distinguish between training and non-training needs
2. Understand the problem or need before designing a solution

3. Save time and money by ensuring that solutions effectively address the problems they are intended to solve

4. Identify factors that will impact training before its development

The evaluation of training, like any other education program, can be beneficial in performing a variety of roles in order to meet various goals of the evaluator. Examples of roles of evaluation process include (Worthen and Sanders 1987, 5):

1. Providing a basis for decisions and policymaking

2. Assess participant achievement

3. Evaluate training program content

4. Improve training materials and programs

Formative and Summative Evaluation

Scriven (1967) first distinguished between the formative and summative roles of evaluation. Formative evaluations, conducted during the implementation of a safety program, provide directors information that helps improve the program. Formative evaluation typically involves content inspection by experts, pilot tests with small numbers of workers, field tests with larger numbers of workers in several plants, and so forth. Each step results in immediate feedback to the developers, who would then use the information to make necessary revisions (Worthen and Sanders 1987, 34).

Summative evaluations are conducted at the end of the program to provide potential consumers with judgments about the safety training program's worth or merit (Worthen and Sanders 1987, 34). For example, after the safety training program is developed, a summative evaluation might be conducted to determine how effective the package is with a national sample of typical facilities, safety managers, and workers. The findings of the summative evaluation would then be made available to others.

Quantitative and Qualitative Evaluation

Because so many people serving in evaluation roles during the late 1950s and 1960s were educational and psychological researchers, it is not surprising that the experimental tradition quickly became the most generally accepted evaluation approach (Worthen and Sanders 1987, 50). Schofield and Anderson (pages 8–9) defined qualitative evaluation as evaluation that:

(a) is conducted in natural settings, such as the factory;

(b) utilizes the researcher as the chief "instrument" in both data-gathering and analysis;

(c) emphasizes "thick description," that is, obtaining "real," "rich," "deep," data which illuminate everyday patterns of action and meaning from the perspective of those being studied;

(d) tends to focus on social processes rather than primarily or exclusively on outcomes;

(e) employs multiple data-gathering methods, especially participant-observation and interviews; and

(f) uses an inductive approach to data analysis, extracting its concepts from the mass of particular detail which constitutes the database.

By contrast, quantitative inquiry generally focuses on the testing of specific hypotheses that are smaller parts of some larger theoretical perspective. This approach follows the traditional natural science model more closely than qualitative research, emphasizing experimental design and statistical methods of analysis. Quantitative research emphasizes standardization, precision, objectivity, and reliability of measurement as well as replicability and generalizability of findings. Thus, quantitative research is characterized not only by a focus on producing numbers but on generating numbers which are suitable for statistical tests (Schofield and Anderson 1984, 8–9).

Objectives-Oriented Evaluation

In objectives-oriented evaluation approach, the purposes of some educational activity are specified, and the evaluation process focuses on the extent to which the objectives have been achieved (Worthen and Sanders 1987, 60). In this type of evaluation, the objectives are established prior to the training. The methods for attaining the objectives are included in the training materials and activities.

When developing the training program, a variety of techniques can be used in the planning process. All of these techniques begin with the development of educational objectives. The objectives specify what is to be learned and how that learning will present itself in observable behaviors. The learning objectives can be classified into one of three categories: cognitive, affective, or psychomotor (Gage and Berliner 1988, 43).

Cognitive objectives deal with intellectual processes such as knowing, recognizing, and thinking. Affective objectives deal with feelings and emotions, while psychomotor objectives deal with skilled ways of moving.

The goal for the trainer is to match the proper training activities to the learning objectives. For example, a classroom instruction method of teaching may be better suited for meeting cognitive objectives while hands-on activities may be a better-suited training method for psychomotor objectives. In any case, the objectives should be established first, and the teaching methods and materials should be developed second.

Finally, evaluation of the training should concentrate on first determining if the educational objectives were met.

Once it has been shown that the educational objectives have been met, further evaluation should be conducted to determine if the training meets the safety program objectives. All too often training is the first method of prevention when in fact another prevention strategy should have been used. An example of this is gathering employees together for a hazard recognition training program after a high frequency of accidents with a piece of equipment. The time and money spent on the training may have been more effectively spent using the engineering approach and properly guarding the unsafe equipment.

The UCLA Evaluation Model

While he was director of the Center for the Study of Evaluation at UCLA, Alkin (1969) developed an evaluation framework that paralleled closely some aspects of the CIPP model. Alkin defined evaluation as "the process of ascertaining the decision areas of concern, selecting appropriate information, and collecting and analyzing information in order to report summary data useful to decision-makers in selecting among alternatives" (Alkin 1969, 2). Alkin's model included the following five types of evaluation (Wothen and Sanders 1987, 81):

1. Systems assessment, to provide information about the state of the system.
2. Program planning, to assist in the selection of particular programs likely to be effective in meeting specific educational needs.
3. Program implementation, to provide information about whether a program was introduced to the appropriate group in the manner intended.
4. Program improvement, to provide information about how a program is functioning, whether interim objectives are being achieved, and whether unanticipated outcomes are appearing.
5. Program certification, to provide information about the value of the program and its potential for use elsewhere.

The Tylerian Evaluation Approach

Tyler conceived a process by which one could determine the extent to which the educational objectives of a training program are being achieved. His approach to the evaluation process were as follows (Worthen and Sanders 1987, 63):

1. Establish broad goals or objectives.
2. Classify the goals or objectives.
3. Define objectives in behavioral terms.

4. Find situations in which achievement of objectives can be shown.
5. Develop or select measurement techniques.
6. Collect performance data.
7. Compare performance data with behaviorally stated objectives.

Discrepancies between performance and objectives would lead to modifications intended to correct the deficiency, and the evaluation cycle would be repeated (Worthen and Sanders 1987, 63).

Expertise-Oriented Evaluation Approach

The expertise-oriented approach to evaluation is one of the oldest and most widely used forms of evaluation (Worthen and Sanders 1987, 98). For example, the worth of a curriculum would be assessed by curriculum or subject-matter experts who would observe the curriculum in action and examine its content and underlying learning theory or in some other way glean sufficient information to render a considered judgment about its value (Worthen and Sanders 1987, 98).

Evaluating Web-Based Training

Internet courses have become an ever-increasing method for meeting safety training needs in the workplace. Web training should be subjected to the same forms of evaluation as other types of training. Comprehensive evaluations of programs should include assessments of students' performances on specified outcomes, instructors' effectiveness, and the quality of courses and the program (Bruce and Hwang 2001, 620).

The most common type of evaluation technique used is student assessment or feedback. Using this assessment of students has found that students' performance in online and traditional classrooms is similar (Bruce and Hwang 2001, 620). These student evaluations provide input as to students' perception about the course, the instruction, and value of the material. Because typical course evaluations are designed for classroom format instruction, additional items may need to be added to traditional student evaluation forms. Areas to include in the evaluation include logistical areas such as ability to access the web page, compatibility of the technology with the students' computer, etc. The purpose of the evaluations is to serve as a basis for improving courses. Instructors can do so by establishing a maintenance folder for each course that includes pertinent evaluations that can be used in further developing a course (Bruce and Hwang 2001, 620).

The next level of evaluation for web-based courses is the overall evaluation of the program. Benchmarking the abilities of students that have completed web-based instruction against students that have completed the same course in a traditional approach is an example of how this type of evaluation may be accomplished.

Improving Training Effectiveness

An important question to answer about the training program is "Was the training program effective?"

Some of the more common reasons for evaluating training include (Phillips 1991, 8):

1. Assess participant satisfaction with the training.
2. Assess the application of the training to the job.
3. Evaluate organizational performance.
4. Test for skills development .

To be most effective, safety training should be tailored to the specific audiences and the specific needs of the organization. Safety personnel can get into a routine where safety training is conducted because the topic has always been given. Additionally, safety training loses its effectiveness when it is being used to solve potential problems that are not rooted in an educational or unsafe act cause. For example, suppose an organization is experiencing accidents caused by the improper physical arrangement of the workspace. Instead of reengineering the workplace, the employees receive training and are expected to prevent the accidents even though they are working in a physical environment that is not conducive to safety.

Another frequent downfall in safety training is improper audience selection for the training program. If the participants do not see a use for the training or the training does not apply to them, one should not expect results from the training program. In the development phase of safety training some key questions to pose when evaluating safety training are (Johnson 1999, p. 104–6):

Is the training specific enough for the intended use?

Can one verify that the training meets the intended use?

Is the training believable to the attendees and is it at the appropriate level?

Are training objectives clearly stated and identifiable?

Is training time reasonable in both timeliness and length of training program?

Summary

Because one of the leading causes for accidents in the workplace is unsafe actions by workers, safety training is an integral part of any accident prevention program. Safety training can and should be analyzed and evaluated in the same manner as any other accident prevention program. In order for workers to know how to work in a safe manner and use their safety training consistently, the safety training needs to be effective.

There are a variety of models available to evaluate the effectiveness of training programs used in the workplace. Some of the approaches include the UCLA Evaluation Model, the Objective-Oriented Evaluation Model, and the Tylerian Evaluation Model. While the approaches may be different, they all have a common goal of providing feedback as to whether a training program is effective.

Chapter Questions

1. Describe three different types of measures that can be used to assess safety training.
2. What are some useful purposes for evaluating safety training?
3. Distinguish between formative and summative evaluation.
4. Distinguish between qualitative and quantitative evaluation.
5. What is the process of designing an objectives-oriented evaluation process?
6. Describe the process for evaluating web-based training programs.
7. Provide an example that utilizes the UCLA model of evaluation.
8. In order to improve the effectiveness of a training program, describe three areas that one would address.
9. Provide an example that utilizes the Tylerian Evaluation Approach.

Assessing the Safety Climate

There are additional safety metrics techniques that can be used to assess the safety climate in an organization in terms of the organization's management, employees, and environment. The environment includes the physical environment, the equipment, and the interfaces between the workers and the work environment. Each area provides the safety professional with additional information to determine if the safety performance in the organization is at an acceptable level.

Perception Surveys

After many years of research with the use of perception survey instruments in the workplace, results indicate that perception surveys are effective in determining the safety climate in an organization. The perception surveys are used to measure attitudes toward and acceptance of safety and health programs (Taggart and Carter 1999, 36). They have been found to be very valuable in determining what needs to be done in the workplace to improve safety. Perception surveys are used to identify the underlying attitudes and beliefs held by management, supervisors, and workers that contribute to accidents. As part of the behavior based safety process, perception surveys are used to determine the extent to which the safety climate in the organization reinforces safe behavior. Often, however, perception surveys find that natural consequences do not reinforce safe behavior; instead, they provide only negative reinforcement for unsafe behavior and this negative reinforcement is provided at very low frequency compared to the undesired behavior (Taggart and Carter 1999, 36). With behavior-based safety and any other performance improvement program introduced into the workplace, these surveys can be used to measure baseline perceptions related to safety and monitor changes in them over a period of time.

Quizzes

Quizzes are a technique that can be used when a safety manager wishes to have employees demonstrate their degree of safety knowledge on a particular subject area. For example, an employee is asked to cut a form on a band saw. The employee is then observed; the examiner notes whether safety glasses were donned, whether the blade guard was adjusted to work height, and whether proper lifting techniques were used (Taggart and Carter 1999, 36). Quizzes are useful in determining a worker's knowledge of a subject matter. The subject matter may be from training or educational classes. Useful outcomes from quizzes include determining the worker's knowledge about certain hazards in the workplace and the OSHA requirements for particular job task.

Discrete Observation of Performance

Discrete observation of employees performing a job task may be an indicator of their knowledge of how to perform the job safely, their ability to perform the job properly, and the attitudes toward safety in general. If an employee is observed performing the job task in an unsafe manner, there are several things that need to be investigated.

First, the extent of the person's knowledge about how to perform the job safely must be determined. A common mistake for supervisors and safety managers is that when they see an employee performing the job in an unsafe manner, they assume the employee knew how to do the job correctly but chose not to perform the job correctly. Education, reeducation, and counseling the employee on the correct way to perform the job task should always be part of the performance improvement process.

Second, if it is determined that the employee knew how to perform the job safely but chose not to, other factors, such as motivators and the employee's attitudes toward working safely, should be explored. Although the employee knew how to perform the job in a safe manner, motivators may be present which reinforce the unsafe behavior.

Third, the employee's attitudes toward safety may be a factor as to why they were observed working in an unsafe manner. If they show they have knowledge on how to perform the job task properly and there are no motivators present for working in an unsafe manner, the employee may have predisposing beliefs about following safety procedures and accident avoidance. Education, positive motivators for working safely, and deterrents for working in an unsafe manner are all performance improvement strategies available to the safety manager.

Economic Analysis

Economic analysis is the process by which the safety manager measures safety performance in terms of financial gains or losses to the organization. It is important to differentiate between intangible outcomes and those that are tangible but difficult to translate into monetary benefits or costs. For example, an investment might decrease pollution, which is very tangible, but it may be difficult to translate this projected reduction to estimated economic gain (Rouse and Boff 1999, 225).

The time value of money is the central concept in this traditional approach. Resources invested now are worth more than the same amounts gained later. This is due to the costs of the investment capital that must be paid, or foregone, while waiting for subsequent returns on the investment. The time value of money is represented by discounting the cash flows produced by the investment to reflect the interest that would, in effect at least, have to be paid on the capital borrowed to finance the investment (Rouse and Boff 1999, 225).

Risk management involves the measurement of financial returns from safety and loss control activities. Risk managers evaluate the costs of implementing safety program activities compared to their costs and the overall savings to the organization in terms of decreased losses and lowered insurance costs. A common approach to this type of evaluation is referred to as cash flow analysis. A seven-step methodology to cost benefit analysis includes the following steps (Rouse and Boff 1999, 225):

Step 1: Identify Stakeholders

The first step involves identifying the stakeholders who are of concern relative to the investments being entertained. This might include, for example, those who will provide the resources that will enable a solution, those who will create the solution, those who will implement the solution, and those who will benefit from the solution.

Step 2: Define Benefit and Cost Attributes

The next step involves defining the benefits and costs involved from the perspective of each stakeholder. These benefits and costs define the attributes of interest to the stakeholders. Usually, a hierarchy of benefits and costs emerges with more abstract concepts at the top (e.g., viability, acceptability, and validity), and concrete measurable attributes at the bottom.

Step 3: Determine Stakeholders' Utility Functions

The value that stakeholders attach to these attributes is defined by stakeholders' utility functions. The utility functions enable mapping disparate benefits and costs to a common scale. A variety of techniques are available for assessing utility functions.

Step 4: Determine Utility Functions Across Stakeholders

Next, one determines how utility functions should be combined across stakeholders. At the very least, this involves assigning relative weights to different stakeholders' utilities. Other considerations such as desires for parity can make the ways in which utilities are combined more complicated.

Step 5: Assess Parameters of Utility Functions

The next step focuses on assessing parameters within the utility models. For example, utility functions that include diminishing or accelerating increments of utility for each increment of benefit or cost involve rate parameters that must be estimated. As another instance, estimates of the weights for multi-stakeholder utility functions have to be estimated. Fortunately, there are varieties of standard methods for making such estimates.

Step 6: Forecast Levels of Attributes

With the cost/benefit model fully defined, one next must forecast levels of attributes or, in other words, benefits and costs. Thus, for each alternative investment, one must forecast the stream of benefits and costs that will result if this investment is made. Quite often, these forecasts involve probability density functions rather than point forecasts. Utility theory models can easily incorporate the impact of such uncertainties on stakeholders' risk aversions. On the other hand, information on probability density functions may not be available, or may be prohibitively expensive. In these situations, beliefs of stakeholders and subject matter experts can be employed, perhaps coupled with sensitivity analysis (see Step 7) to determine where additional data collection may be warranted.

Step 7: Calculate Expected Utilities

The final step involves calculating the expected utility of each alternative investment. This step also involves using sensitivity analysis to assess, for example, the extent to which the rank ordering of alternatives, by overall utility, changes as parameters and attribute levels of the model are varied.

Program Logic Model Framework

The Program Logic Framework can be used to organize planning and analysis during program design or when designing outcomes-based evaluations of the programs (McNamara 2000, 1). The model serves as a framework for evaluating major program functions and how they relate to organizational resources, client needs, and the organizational goals. This model has been applied in a variety of fields, including public health, education, and safety. To use the model, a process flow evaluation approach is employed, beginning with the inputs into the organization and ending with the outcomes.

Inputs into the organization are anything the organization brings in for processing, which can include people, equipment, and raw materials. Once in the organization, the processes that are used upon the inputs are examined. Depending upon the type of organization, processes can include production processes, training, education, and any other types of services.

Outputs are the results of the process. If applied to a manufacturing process, the outputs are the products. In a service industry, the output would be the service provided. In the final stage of the program logic model, outcomes are addressed on three levels. Depending upon their impact and longevity, they are classified as short term, intermediate, or long term. At each step of the logic model framework, performance improvement strategies can be implemented with the goal of continual improvement in the process of providing goods or services and in the quality of the outcomes attained.

Systems Safety Techniques

Systems safety techniques have been proven a valuable process for assessing the reliability and safety of complex systems. There are a variety of techniques that can be used to identify potential problem areas of the system. The major components of a system include the equipment, the personnel, and the environment. The systems safety techniques can be used before the fact to identify potential situations that can increase the risk for a failure, or they can be used in after-the-fact situations to determine the contributing factors that led to the accident, thus identifying prevention areas for future accidents.

Techniques used in systems safety frequently have specific goals and areas that they can address. For example, some techniques are used to analyze the hardware and equipment aspects of the system while other techniques are used to assess the human aspect. From a safety metrics standpoint, systems safety techniques can be used to identify areas for improvement in the organization. While there are hundreds of system safety techniques available, some of the more commonly used are Fault Tree Analysis (FTA), Procedure Analysis, Failure Modes and Effects Analysis, and Root Cause Analysis.

Fault Tree Analysis

Fault Tree Analysis was one of the earliest systems safety techniques developed for examining equipment failures. Fault Tree Analysis is a top down procedure that identifies undesirable events and their contributing factors. Once a tree has been developed, probabilities of failures can be determined for individual components in the tree. With the individual probabilities, overall probabilities of failures and can be calculated for event paths using Boolean algebra.

Procedure Analysis

Procedure analysis can be used to examine the steps in a procedure or task. Procedure analysis requires the task to be broken down into individual steps. For each step, the hazards are identified and control measures for each hazard determined. Procedure analysis can be expanded to include the use of reliabilities for individual steps that can be ultimately used to determine over all reliability for completing the job task. This procedure can also be referred to as a Job Safety Analysis. The completed analyses are used to determine safe job procedures, the need for personal protection equipment, and the need for engineering controls.

Failure Modes and Effects Analysis

Failure Modes and Effects Analysis (FMEA) examines systems, element by element (Systems Safety Society 1997, 3-111). The analysis procedure requires the identification of the individual components that make up the system under examination. With the components identified, the modes in which the component failures as well as the effects that that failure has upon the system are determined. A further step to the FMEA procedure is the examination of the risk associated with the failure. The risk, also referred to as criticality, provides the investigators with a method of ranking the hazards in the system and providing a method for prioritization of hazards.

Root Cause Analysis

Root Cause Analysis focuses on why the investigation findings occurred rather than the specifics of the findings. The purpose of the Root Cause Analysis is to identify causal factors relating to a mishap or near-miss incidents. The technique goes beyond the direct causes to identify fundamental reasons for the fault or failure (Systems Safety Society 1997, 3-235). The objective is to find one root cause that is the fundamental reason behind a set of related deficiencies, shortcomings, or observations. By emphasizing a few root causes, management can correct a wide variety of deficiencies or faults in a system. The Root Cause Analysis technique is used primarily for failure analyses and other investigations. Using the accident cause categories from the management oversight risk tree (MORT), "why" statements are arranged into surface and root cause categories. Examples of the MORT categories of surface cause categories include amelioration, communications, training, and human factors, to name a few (Systems Safety Society 1997, 3-235).

The Balanced Scorecard

The Balanced Scorecard is a new approach to strategic management, developed in the early 1990s by Drs. Robert Kaplan and David Norton (Balanced Scorecard Institute 2001). The concept "translates" the planning perspective of an institution (mission, strategic vision, and goals) into a system of performance indicators that covers all-important perspectives of performance (i.e., finances, users, internal processes, and improvement activities) (Poll 2001, 709).

The balanced scorecard management system provides feedback concerning internal business processes and external outcomes. To improve performance, continuous improvement strategies are incorporated into the model. The process involves a defining the mission and goals for the organization. As with other performance improvement processes, the activities necessary to meet the goals are developed and measures indicative of that performance identified. Continual improvement is incorporated into the model which balances financial and non-financial demands of the organization with performance.

Summary

For a safety program to be effective, the safety climate needs to be supportive of the program. The safety climate includes management, workers, the physical equipment in the workplace, and the interfaces between the people and the environment. Perception surveys can be used to assess the status of the safety climate in the workplace. Key areas that perception surveys can assess include management support for safety and employees' attitudes and beliefs about safety. Environmental conditions and interfaces between equipment and workers can be assessed using various system safety techniques. Examples of system safety techniques include root cause analysis and failure modes and effects analysis.

Chapter Questions

1. Describe the uses of perception surveys for the purpose of measuring safety performance.

2. How would one implement a safety performance measurement program that utilizes discrete observation?

3. How can economic analysis be used to assess safety performance?

4. What is risk management and how can it be used in a safety performance assessment program?

5. In the methodology for cost benefit analysis, the first step is identifying stakeholders. How would one go about completing this step?

6. What is systems safety and how can it be used to assess safety performance?

7. Describe fault tree analysis and how the procedure can be used to assess safety performance.

8. Describe root cause analysis and how the procedure can be used to assess safety performance.

9. What impact has the military had upon systems safety?

10. Describe the Balanced Scorecard management system and explain how it can be used to assess safety performance.

Performance Indices

There are numerous safety metrics available to safety and health professionals that can be used as performance indicators. These metrics include those established by the Occupational Safety and Health Administration, the Department of Energy, and private industry. These resources provide the safety professional with methodologies to measure safety performance and serve as benchmark indicators.

OSHA-Based Incidence Rates

Occupational Safety and Health Administration (OSHA) incidence rates are one of the more common methods of measuring safety performance. Incidence rates for higher levels of industry detail are produced using aggregated, weighted, and benchmarked totals. Rates may be computed using industry, employment size, geographic area, extent or outcome of case, and case characteristic category. Rates for illnesses and rates for case characteristic categories are published per 10,000 full-time employees, using 20,000,000 hours instead of 200,000 hours in the formula shown below. Rates per 10,000 workers can be converted to rates per 100 workers by moving the decimal point left two places and rounding the resulting rate to the nearest tenth. There are varieties of formulas that can be used to calculate these incidence rates. Some of the more common rates are the OSHA recordable injury incidence rate, the recordable illness incidence rate, the death rate, and the lost day case injury rate. The formulas used to calculate these rates are as follows:

$$\text{OSHA Recordable Injury Incidence rate} = \frac{(\text{Number of Recordable Injuries}) \times 200,000}{\text{Number of hours worked}}$$

$$\text{OSHA Recordable Illness Incidence rate} = \frac{(\text{Number of Recordable Illnesses}) \times 200,000}{\text{Number of hours worked}}$$

$$\text{Death rate} = \frac{(\text{Number of Deaths}) \times 200,000}{\text{Number of hours worked}}$$

$$\text{OSHA Lost Day Injury Case rate} = \frac{(\text{Number of Lost Day Cases}) \times 200{,}000}{\text{Number of hours worked}}$$

The OSHA incidence rates are based upon 200,000 hours of exposure—equivalent to a company with 100 employees, each working 2,000 hours in a calendar year. This corresponds to what an "average" full-time employee would work in a 40-hour week during a 52-week year (minus two weeks for vacation and holidays). Using this exposure value of 200,000 hours allows for comparisons between "equal" 100 full-time employee establishments. These comparisons can be made between different establishments and comparisons within the same establishment between different subgroups. Comparisons can also be made between the establishment's OSHA incidence rate and national estimates of incidence rates based upon Standard Industrial Classification (SIC) Codes and the new North American Industry Classification System (NAICS).

OSHA's Gravity-Based Penalty System

For some larger corporations with multiple establishments, a method of quantifying safety performance has been through the tracking of Occupational Safety and Health Administration (OSHA) violations and penalties. The Occupational Safety and Health Administration uses a gravity-based penalty (GBP) system to establish the initial penalty for violations. (However, some penalties, such as recordkeeping violations, are set by regulations.) This weighting scheme has two primary advantages. 1) By giving greater weight to hazards that are more likely to cause injury/illness and those likely to cause more-serious injury/illness, the checklist score will provide a better indication of true conditions within the plant. 2) By assigning a dollar value to hazards detected, management will more likely recognize financial benefits of safety programs and, thus enable rapid abatement (United States Department of Labor, Occupational Safety and Health Administration 2001).

The gravity-based penalty system establishes the initial penalty based upon the potential severity of loss the hazard poses and the probability that an injury or illness could occur because of the alleged violation. The severity assessment classifies the alleged violations as serious or other-than-serious. The severity assessment is assigned to a hazard to be cited according to the most serious injury or illness which could reasonably be expected to result from an employee's exposure as follows (United States Department of Labor, Occupational Safety and Health Administration 2001):

(1) **High Severity:** Death from injury or illness; injuries involving permanent disability; or chronic, irreversible illnesses.

(2) **Medium Severity:** Injuries or temporary, reversible illnesses resulting in hospital-ization or a variable but limited period of disability.

(3) **Low Severity:** Injuries or temporary, reversible illnesses not resulting in hospital-ization and requiring only minor supportive treatment.

(4) **Minimal Severity:** Other-than-serious violations. Although such violations reflect conditions that have a direct and immediate relationship to the safety and health of employees, the injury or illness most likely to result would probably not cause death or serious physical harm.

The next step requires a probability assessment be conducted for the hazard. The probability that an injury or illness will result from a hazard has no role in determin-ing the classification of a violation, but does affect the amount of the penalty. The probability is categorized either as greater or as lesser probability, defined as follows:

(a) Greater probability results when the likelihood that an injury or illness will occur is judged to be relatively high.

(b) Lesser probability results when the likelihood that an injury or illness will occur is judged to be relatively low.

In addition, there are penalty factors that may reduce the penalty from the initial gravity-based level. The three factors are (United States Department of Labor, Occu-pational Safety and Health Administration 2001):

1.   The size of the business
2.   The good faith of the employer
3.   The employer's history of previous violations

The GBP may be reduced by as much as 95 per cent depending upon the employer's good faith, size of business, and history of previous violations. Up to a 60-percent reduction is permitted for size, up to a 25-percent reduction for good faith, and up to a 10-percent reduction for history.

Bureau of Labor Statistics' Occupational Safety and Health Statistics

When the Occupational Safety and Health Act of 1970 was signed into law, the Bureau of Labor Statistics was given the responsibility of keeping track of the occupational fatali-ties and illnesses in the United States. The Bureau of Labor Statistics annually reports on the number of workplace injuries, illnesses, and fatalities. Such information is useful in identifying industries with high rates or large numbers of injuries, illnesses, and fatalities both nationwide and separately for those states participating in this program.

Summary data on nonfatal injuries and illnesses are released first that identify the number and rate of injuries and illnesses by industry. After more analysis is completed, case and demographic data provide additional details on the worker injured, the nature of the disabling condition, and the event and source producing that condition for those cases that involve one or more days away from work. Fatality data provides information on 28 separate data elements including information on the worker, the fatal incident, and the machinery or equipment involved.

Bureau of Labor Statistics Handbook of Methods

The Bureau of Labor Statistics Handbook of Methods provides detailed information on the various statistical and sampling procedures the Bureau of Labor Statistics uses to summarize the incidence of occupational injuries, illnesses, and fatalities in the United States. The Bureau of Labor Statistics has been collecting this type of data since the 1940s. However, it wasn't until the passage of the Occupational Safety and Health Act of 1970 when the Bureau of Labor Statistics was given the responsibility of developing a formal data collection and analysis system (Bureau of Labor Statistics 1997, 71).

The Handbook is divided in chapters for each of the major programs for which the BLS has data collection and analysis responsibilities. Chapter 9, Occupational Safety and Health Statistics is divided into two major subdivisions: Survey of Occupational Injuries and Illnesses, and Census of Fatal Occupational Injuries.

The Bureau of Labor Statistics uses a variety of statistics to report the occupational injury and illness experience in the United States. The number of injuries and illnesses are reported nationwide and by industry for three basic types of cases (United States Department of Labor, Bureau of Labor Statistics 1997):

- Lost workday cases
- Days-away-from-work cases
- Nonfatal cases without lost workdays

Days-away-from-work cases, which may also involve restricted workdays, are a subset of lost workday cases, which include days-away-from-work cases and cases involving restricted work activity only (Bureau of Labor Statistics 1997, 72).

In addition to injury and illness counts, the survey also reports on the frequency (incidence rate) of such cases (Bureau of Labor Statistics 1997, 72). The BLS uses a standard of 200,000 man-hours of annual exposure when calculating rates. The number 200,000 is equivalent to 100 workers working 40 hours per week for 50 weeks during the year. Using rates allows for comparisons across industries and across organizations of differing sizes. These rates also are useful in evaluating the safety performance of a particular industry over time or in comparing state-to-state variations in an industry's safety record (Bureau of Labor Statistics 1997, 72).

Survey of Occupational Injuries and Illnesses

The BLS administers an annual Survey of Occupational Injuries and Illnesses. The survey is an indication as to the levels of occupational injuries and illnesses occurring in the United States. Under the Occupational Safety and Health Act of 1970, most private employers are now required to record related injuries and illnesses as part of the recordkeeping standards. If selected through the random selection process, employers are required to submit their occupational injury and illness information to the Bureau of Labor Statistics for the purpose of compiling national estimates on the extent of injuries and illnesses in the workplace.

Census of Fatal Occupational Injuries

A comprehensive source for data concerning occupational fatalities is maintained by the Bureau of Labor Statistics' (BLS) Census of Fatal Occupational Injuries (CFOI). The CFOI is an official, systematic, verifiable count of fatal occupational injuries that occur during the year (Bureau of Labor Statistics 1997). It has been adopted by the National Safety Council and other organizations as the authoritative source for a count of fatal work injuries in the United States.

To ensure that the fatalities are work-related, cases are substantiated with two or more source documents or a source document and a follow-up questionnaire (Bureau of Labor Statistics 1997). This data is an excellent resource for establishing benchmarks and performance measures for occupational fatalities.

DOE Occupational Injury/Illness Indices

The Department of Energy and its contractor injury and illness indicators include occupational injury and illness rates per 200,000 work hours for total recordable cases, lost workday cases, lost workdays, and occupational illnesses. In addition, the DOE has developed two measures used to quantify occupational injuries and illnesses. These measures are the ratio of Lost Workdays to Lost Workday Cases and the DOE Safety Cost Index (Training Resources and Data Exchange [TRADE] 1995, 1-60–61).

The ratio of lost workdays to lost workday cases represents a severity measure for the injuries and illnesses. The higher the ratio, the more days missed per case. The ratio is calculated using the following formula:

$$\text{Ratio of Lost Workdays to Lost Workday Cases} = \frac{\text{Number of Lost Workdays}}{\text{Number of Lost Workday Cases}}$$

Another performance indicator used by the Department of Energy is the DOE Cost Index. The cost index applies a weighting factor to the frequency of injury and illness cases. The more severe the outcome of the case, the greater the weighting factor. The coefficients are weighting factors, which take into account factors such as dollar costs analyses and cost-benefit analyses. The index is approximately equal to cents lost per hour worked. The DOE Cost Index is computed as follows (Training Resources and Data Exchange [TRADE] 1995, 1-60–61):

$$\text{Cost Index} = \frac{100(1{,}000{,}000\,D + 500{,}000\,T + 2{,}000\,LWC + 1{,}000\,WDL + 400\,WDLR + 2{,}000\,NFC)}{\text{Total Work - Hours}}$$

Where:

D = The number of deaths.

T = The number of permanent transfers or terminations due to occupational illness or injury.

LWC = The number of lost workday cases.

WDL = The number of days away from work.

WDLR = The number of restricted workdays.

NFC = The number of non-fatal cases without days away from work or restricted workdays.

An example of this index in use is as follows:

An organization experienced the following during one calendar year in which there were 760,500 man-hours worked:

Category Symbol	Category of Occupational Injury, Illness, etc.	Experience
D	Number of deaths	1
T	Number of permanent transfers or terminations due to occupational illness or injury.	3
LWC	Number of lost workday cases.	4
WDL	Number of days away from work.	15
WDLR	Number of restricted workdays.	23
NFC	Number of non-fatal cases without days away from work or restricted workdays.	1

$$\text{Cost Index} = \frac{100\left[(1{,}000{,}000 \times 1) + (500{,}000 \times 3) + (2{,}000 \times 4) + (1{,}000 \times 15) + (400 \times 23) + (2{,}000 \times 1)\right]}{760{,}500}$$

Cost Index = 333.22

This index value indicates that for every hour worked, the organization lost $3.33 due to occupational injuries, deaths, and lost workdays. This index value can be compared to other organizations, and from year to year. With some idea as to what an "acceptable" index value is, it can be used to benchmark safety performance.

Six Sigma's Capability Index

Six Sigma is a highly structured program for improving business processes involving an intense effort to reduce process variation to a minimum, so that processes consistently meet or exceed customer expectations and requirements (Pyzdek 2001, 19). Six Sigma is a disciplined methodology of measuring and improving the quality of an organization's products and processes with the goal of eliminating all defects. General Electric, one of the early adopters of Six Sigma, uses the program as a quality objective that specifies the variability required of a process, in terms of product specifications, to improve quality and reliability.

While Six Sigma was originally used for developing continuous improvement programs related to production, many of its management structure components and methodologies can be applied to safety performance improvement in the workplace. One useful measure frequently used in Six Sigma is the capability index.

The Capability Index

The Capability Index (Cpk) is a measure of how well the process is in control—or otherwise stated, free from defects or departures from what can be statistically considered "normal." The Capability Index tells you if the process is truly capable of meeting the outcomes requirements.

The Capability Index (Cpk) is calculated as follows (Juran and Godfrey 1999, 22.18):

$$Cpk = \frac{\text{Minimum of the } Z_L \text{ or } Z_U}{3}$$

Where:

$$Z_L = \frac{\text{Mean} - \text{LSL}}{\text{Standard Deviation}}$$

$$Z_U = \frac{\text{USL} - \text{Mean}}{\text{Standard Deviation}}$$

And:

Z_U is the Upper Process Location
Z_L is the Lower Process Location
USL   is the Upper Specification Limit
LSL   is the Lower Specification Limit

To calculate the Capability Index for a process, information about the process must be known including an acceptable average, upper and lower specification limits, and the knowledge that the process is in statistical control. An acceptable value for Z_L and Z_U is 3.00 or greater. Referring to a Z table, a Z_U value of 3.00 indicates that approximately .1% of the readings will be above the upper limit while a Z_L value of 3.00 indicates that approximately .1% of the readings will be below the lower limit.

Applying Six Sigma Process Capability to Safety

Suppose data was collected for an organization pertaining to a ventilation system designed to maintain air quality in a painting operation. With the system operating, data over the past three months indicated that the airborne lead levels averaged 19.98 ppm with a standard deviation of .02 ppm. The safety manager wishes to maintain the air levels at 20.0 ppm while engineering design data on the air handling system indicates that it is capable of maintaining air lead levels within .01 ppm.

The first step is to establish the upper and lower specification for the air handling system. The Upper Specification Level is the upper acceptable tolerance level for the air handling system. In this example, the desired average level is 20 ppm while the system is designed to maintain that level plus or minus .01 ppm. The Upper Specification Level is determined using the desired average level of 20 ppm + .01 ppm = 20.01 ppm while the Lower Specification Level would be 20 ppm − .01 ppm = 19.99 ppm.

The Upper Process Location (Z_U) is calculated using:

$$Z_U = \frac{USL - Mean}{Standard\ Deviation}$$

or

$$Z_U = \frac{20.01 - 19.98}{.02} = 1.5$$

The obtained Z_U value of 1.5 is unacceptable since a minimum value of 3.0 is desired. A Z_U value of 1.5 indicates, using a Z table, that approximately 7% of the readings are expected to be above the upper specification level of 20.01 ppm.

The Lower Process Location (Z_L) is calculated using:

$$Z_L = \frac{Mean - LSL}{Standard\ Deviation}$$

or

$$Z_L = \frac{19.98 - 19.99}{.02} = -.5$$

A Z_L value of $-.5$ indicates, using a Z table, that approximately 30% of the readings would be below the lower specification level, which in this example, would indicate that exposure to the air contaminants would be even less than expected.

The next step is to determine the Capability Index (Cpk) for the system. Cpk is calculated by using the smaller value of either the Upper Process Location (Z_U) or Lower Process Location (Z_L). In this example, Z_L is the smaller value with $-.5$, therefore, the Process Capability (Cpk) is calculated and interpreted as follows:

$$Cpk = \frac{-.5}{3} = -.16$$

Since the result of $-.16$ is less than 1.00, which is required, and 1.33, which is preferred, the Capability Index indicates that the air handling equipment is not capable of meeting the requirements of controlling the air contaminant levels to a sufficient level as defined by the process specifications. In approximately 37% of the samples would be expected to be outside of the desired upper and lower specification ranges. While the lower readings in this example would be beneficial, the readings above the upper level could pose increased risks.

Summary

A number of safety performance indices are available to the safety manager for measuring safety performance. In previous chapters, measures of safe behaviors, insurance indices, and training program effectiveness were presented. This chapter presented performance indices from a variety of organizations. The Occupational Safety and Health Administration's incidence rates measure rates of death, lost workdays, and incidents. To quantify the severity of a hazard, OSHA uses a penalty system that is based on the potential severity of the injury that can occur and the probability that a worker can come into contact with the hazard. Other performance indices include the Bureau of Labor Statistics' measures and the Department of Energy's Safety Cost Index. All of these indices provide the safety manager with techniques for quantifying safety performance; they also allow for benchmarking against other organizations that use these same indices.

Chapter Questions

1. The exposure number of 200,000 man-hours represents what in an OSHA incidence rate?
2. What purpose do rates serve?

3. A company experienced 15 OSHA recordable injuries over a year. The organization accumulated 1,220,000 man-hours. What is the OSHA recordable injury rate?

4. When calculating penalties, OSHA may reduce the penalty because of what factors?

5. What role does the Census of Fatal Occupational Injuries play in national statistics?

6. How is the DOE's ratio of lost workdays to lost workday cases calculated?

7. What does the DOE's Cost Index approximate?

Voluntary Performance Standards

Safety professionals can draw upon voluntary standards and national consensus standards to develop safety performance programs, implement continuous improvement programs related to safety, and develop measures of safety performance. National consensus standards are developed through a process of obtaining input from industry representatives on the development of the standard. This representation can include manufacturers, trade associations, professional organizations, as well as other standards development bodies in the United States, in other countries, or from international coalitions such as the European Community.

Voluntary standards can include standards that followed a national consensus approach and other industry standards that did not obtain a national consensus. Voluntary standards can also include standards of safety performance developed by a professional organization or a company.

Some of the most prominent voluntary and national consensus standard organizations include the American National Standards Institute (ANSI), American Society for Testing and Materials (ASTM), and the American Society of Mechanical Engineers (ASME). The major international organization that has the primary mission of developing international standards is the International Organization for Standardization (ISO).

While national consensus and voluntary standards may not be enforceable, unless a regulatory agency adopts them, such as OSHA, they still serve as a recognized acceptable level of performance. In some cases, the national consensus standards may be viewed as the minimum acceptable level of safety performance.

OSHA's Voluntary Performance Standards

The Occupational Safety and Health Administration's Voluntary Protection Programs (VPP) emphasize the importance of worksite safety and health programs in meeting the goal of the Occupational Safety and Health Act, "to assure so far as possible every working man and woman in the nation safe and healthful working conditions. . . ." (United States Department of Labor). Employers that participate in the Voluntary Protection Programs (VPP) have recognized that an effective safety and health program affects the bottom line (Garner and Horn 2000, 31). The criteria can be used by any organization regardless of size or industry.

According to OSHA's semiannual regulatory agenda, "Worksite-specific safety and health programs are increasingly being recognized as the most effective way of reducing job-related accidents, injuries and illnesses" (Garner and Horn 2000, 31). The VPP criteria lends itself well to performance improvement. It provides measurable activities that have been shown to improve safety performance. The criteria for the VPP Program can be found in *OSHA's Directive TED 8.1a—Revised Voluntary Protection Programs (VPP) Policies and Procedures Manual* (1996).

Benefits of VPP

Organizations that use OSHA's VPP criteria as guidelines for safety performance improvement in the workplace experience a number of benefits. Some of the benefits of participation in the VPP program include (United States Department of Labor 1996):

* Participants are not subject to routine OSHA inspections, because OSHA's VPP onsite reviews ensure that their safety and health programs provide superior protection.

* Establishing and maintaining safety and health programs on the VPP model are reflected in substantially lower than average worker injury rates at VPP worksites.

* Injury Incidence Rates: In 1994, of the 178 companies in the program, 9 sites had no injuries at all. Overall, the sites had only 45% of the injuries expected, or were 55% below the expected average for similar industries.

* Lost Workday Injury Rates: In 1994, of the 178 companies in the program, 31 had no lost workday injuries. Overall, the sites had only 49% of the lost workdays expected, or were 51% below the expected average for similar industries.

* While protecting workers from occupational safety and health hazards, companies following the management guidelines mandated for VPP membership also experience decreased costs in workers' compensation and lost work time, and often experience increased production and improved employee morale.

* Documentation of these assertions come from testimony given by safety and health managers during OSHA hearings on the Safety and Health Program Management Guidelines, from triennial reports of member sites, and from the literature cited.

VPP Onsite Evaluation Format for Safety and Health Programs

The following criteria cover all participant VPP sites (United States Department of Labor 1996) which appear in *OSHA's Directive TED 8.1a - Revised Voluntary Protection Programs (VPP) Policies and Procedures Manual* (1996). These areas can be useful for an organization to assist in establishing benchmarks and areas for performance measurement.

1. **Management Leadership and Employee Involvement.**

Management demonstrates commitment to safety and health protection by establishing policies and results-oriented objectives for worker safety, establishing goals for the safety and health programs and objectives for meeting that goal, communicating goals and objectives, and integrating authority and responsibility for safety and health.

2. **Management commitment to maintaining the VPP requirements.**

Management demonstrates commitment to the safety program by meeting VPP safety program requirements.

3. **Safety and Health Program Planning.**

Management demonstrates safety and health program planning by including safety and health in the planning processes.

4. **Written Safety and Health Program.**

A written program should include critical elements such as management leadership and employee involvement, worksite analysis, hazard prevention and control, and safety and health training. Sub-elements of a basic safety and health program should also be part of the written program.

5. **Top Management Leadership.**

Top management should display leadership in implementing the safety and health program. This includes establishing clear lines of communication with employees, setting an example of safe and healthful behavior, and ensuring that all workers at the site, including contract workers, continue to be provided equal high quality safety and health protection.

6. **Employee Involvement.**

Employees are actively involved in the development and implementation of safety program activities. Employees are aware of the of VPP program, rights, etc.

There should be meaningful employee involvement that impacts decision-making and evidence seen by the team that the method has been effective.

The Joint Labor-Management Committee. A joint labor-management committee should be used in general industry. Employee members appear to have management duties as regular work assignments.

Construction Industry only: Do all committee members work full-time at the site?
Have employees been involved in the selection procedures?
Have committee members been given training regarding their responsibility?
How frequently has the committee met?
What is the committee's role, in inspections, accident investigations?
What is the effectiveness of committee efforts?

7. **Contract Workers.**

For General Industry: How does the written program cover contract workers who are intermingled with the applicant's employees?

For Construction: How does the written program provide for control of safety and health conditions for other contractors and subcontractor employees?

What evidence have you seen that all contract employees employed at the site are still covered by the same quality safety and health protection?

8. **Authority and Resources.**

Is proper authority still being given so that assigned safety and health responsibilities can be met? Are adequate resources including staff, equipment, and promotions still committed to workplace safety and health?

9. **Line Accountability.**

Has the system for holding managers, supervisors, and employees accountable changed since the last onsite evaluation? If so, how? Is this as effective as it was at the last onsite evaluation? Are authority and responsibility for safety and health still clearly defined in the written program? Has this been adequately implemented?

10. **Safety and Health Program Evaluation.**

Does the annual evaluation cover and assess the effectiveness of all aspects of the safety and health program, including the elements described above and any other elements?

Worksite Analysis

As part of the VPP process, worksites are evaluated to determine if the VPP program requirements are being met and that safety has been integrated into the overall functioning of the organization. The following are components of the VPP general safety program (US Dept. of Labor 1996):

- Planning and integration of safety
- Job monitoring systems, hazard analysis systems
- Site inspections programs with follow-up
- Hazard recognition training
- Employee hazard reporting system and follow-up
- Written accident/incident investigation reporting system in place with follow-up
- System to analyze injury and illness trends over time through a review of injury/illness experience hazards identified through inspections, employee reports, and accident investigations

Applying OSHA's VPP Criteria to a Safety Metrics Program

The Occupational Safety and Health Administration's VPP Program criteria can be used to establish safety performance measures for the workplace. The requirements are activity-based, which means they are easily applied to a monitoring and assessment program. The safety metrics could consist of monitoring and recording whether the activities have been conducted.

As part of the VPP program, an evaluation process should be established to determine if the activities have been completed and assess how effective the activities have been in preventing accidents and minimizing losses. Finally, the VPP criteria also establish guidelines for conducting surveys of the worksites and interviewing employees; while these guidelines were designed for OSHA personnel to follow, safety personnel can also use them to conduct worksite evaluations. Remember that although the VPP criteria are the minimum for the workplace, they can be used as a starting point and expanded using a variety of other activity-based safety measures.

With these activity-based performance measures, there is also a variety of safety metrics that can be used to assess program performance. As identified by OSHA in studies of VPP organizations, OSHA injury incidence rates, lost work day rates, and workers' compensation losses are a few safety metrics that have been correlated to the performance of the VPP criteria activities. These measures can easily be expanded to include unsafe behaviors, accident trends, and near misses.

American National Standards Institute

The American National Standards Institute (ANSI) promotes the use of U.S. standards internationally, advocates U.S. policy and technical positions in international and regional standards organizations, and encourages the adoption of international standards as national standards where these meet the needs of the user community (American National Standards Institute 2001). ANSI is the sole U.S. representative and dues-paying member of the two major non-treaty international standards organizations, the International Organization for Standardization (ISO), and, via the U.S. National Committee (USNC), the International Electrotechnical Commission (IEC) (American National Standards Institute 2001).

American Society of Mechanical Engineers

Founded in 1880 as the American Society of Mechanical Engineers, today ASME International is a nonprofit educational and technical organization serving a worldwide membership of 125,000. The goals of ASME are to promote and enhance the technical competency and professional well-being of members, and through quality programs and activities in mechanical engineering, better enable its practitioners to contribute to the well-being of humankind (American Society of Mechanical Engineers 2002).

AMSE conducts one of the world's largest technical publishing operations, holds some 30 technical conferences and 200 professional development courses each year. ASME is responsible for many industrial and manufacturing standards.

National Fire Protection Association

NFPA has been a worldwide leader in providing fire, electrical, and life safety to the public since 1896 (NFPA 2002). The mission of the international nonprofit organization is to reduce the worldwide burden of fire and other hazards on the quality of life by providing and advocating scientifically based consensus codes and standards, research, training and education (NFPA 2002). The NFPA publishes of the *National Electrical Code,* the *Life Safety Code,* and 300 other codes and standards through a full, open-consensus process (NFPA 2002).

American Society for Testing Materials

ASTM International is a not-for-profit organization that provides a forum for the development and publication of voluntary consensus standards for materials, products, systems, and services (ASTM 2000). More than 20,000 members representing producers, users, ultimate consumers, and representatives of government and academia develop documents that serve as a basis for manufacturing, procurement, and regulatory activities. ASTM publishes standard test methods, specifications, practices, guides, classifications and terminology for materials, products, systems, and services (ASTM 2000).

International Organization for Standardization

The International Organization for Standardization, commonly referred to as ISO, is a non-governmental organization founded in 1947 with headquarters in Geneva, Switzerland (ISO 2001). It is a federation of national standards bodies from some 130 countries, one body from each country. Its mission is to promote the development of standardization and related activities in the world with a view to facilitating the international exchange of goods and services and to developing co-operation in the spheres of intellectual property, scientific, technological, and economic activity. ISO's work results in international agreements, which are published as international standards (Oluoch-Wauna and Lucas O. 2001, 4). One note about the term "ISO" is that many believe ISO is an acronym for the organization, which it is not. The term 'ISO' is a word derived from the Greek isos, meaning "equal."

ISO is structured into approximately 180 technical committees (TCs) each of which specialize in drafting standards in a particular area. In 1979, ISO formed Technical Committee 176 (TC 176) to develop global standards for quality management and quality assurance systems. ISO/TC 176 is the "umbrella" committee under which the ISO 9000 series of quality management and quality assurance standards are being developed (International Organization for Standardization Technical Committee 176 2001).

Using Voluntary and National Consensus Standards in a Safety Metrics Program

Voluntary and national consensus standards can be very useful in the development and implementation of a safety performance improvement program. These standards can serve two purposes: first, national consensus standards can provide an accepted management structure for the safety performance program, and second, national consensus standards can serve as a basis for establishing acceptable safety performance levels and a means for measuring safety performance.

National consensus standards such as ISO 9000:2000 and ISO 14000 have a management structure component to them which can easily be adapted to a safety performances improvement program. For example, instead of using ISO 9000:2000 to focus on a quality product, a safety management structure can be established to focus on a safe work environment. With the safety management system developed and documented, attention can then be directed to the continuous improvement processes in the organization. Activities in implementing the improvement process as it pertains to safety includes identifying data needs, collecting safety performance data, comparing the data against benchmarks, and implementing control measures to improve safety performance.

National consensus standards can be used to formulate performance levels and safety metrics. Because the standards are already developed, and most cases viewed as an industry-accepted level of performance, the safety manager may choose to adopt the standards—thus eliminating the need to create new performance measures. Because the national consensus standards have been adopted as acceptable performance within an industry, the additional burden of having to validate acceptability has also been addressed through the standards development process.

Summary

There are numerous safety organizations and professional standards bodies that have developed voluntary and national consensus standards. The safety manager can adapt these consensus standards to establish safety performance standards in the workplace. Some examples of sources for standards that can be applied to safety performance programs include the American National Standards Institute, National Fire Protection Association, and the International Organization for Standardization. These organizations and others publish thousands of safety standards that can be incorporated into any safety performance program.

Chapter Questions

1. What does VPP represent?
2. Describe the benefits of cooperating with OSHA in the VPP program.
3. Describe some of the benefits of participating in OSHA's VPP program.
4. Describe the components of a safety program that would indicate management leadership and involvement.
5. How can OSHA's VPP program criteria be used to improve safety performance?
6. Describe the process of participating in OSHA's VPP program.
7. Describe the components of a safety program that would indicate line accountability.
8. Describe five areas that would be evaluated during the worksite analysis of the VPP program.
9. What provisions for contract workers should be made?
10. Describe the components of a safety program that would indicate acceptable safety and health training.
11. Differentiate between national consensus standards and voluntary standards.
12. Describe the American National Standards Institute's role in developing consensus standards.

Appendix A

Control Chart Table

Table of Factors for Computing Control Charts

(Copyright ASTM. Reprinted with Permission)

Observations in Sample n	CHART FOR AVERAGES			CHART FOR STANDARD DEVIATIONS						CHART FOR RANGES						
	Factors For Control Limits			Factors For Central Line		Factors For Control Limits				Factors For Central Line		Factors For Control Limits				
	A	A_2	A_3	C_4	$1/C_4$	B_3	B_4	B_5	B_6	d_2	$1/d_2$	d_3	D_1	D_2	D_3	D_4
2	2.121	1.880	2.659	0.7979	1.2533	0	3.267	0	2.606	1.128	0.8862	0.853	0	3.686	0	3.267
3	1.732	1.023	1.954	0.8862	1.1284	0	2.568	0	2.276	1.693	0.5908	0.888	0	4.358	0	2.575
4	1.500	0.729	1.628	0.9213	1.0854	0	2.266	0	2.088	2.059	0.4857	0.880	0	4.698	0	2.282
5	1.342	0.577	1.427	0.9400	1.0638	0	2.089	0	1.964	2.326	0.4299	0.864	0	4.918	0	2.114
6	1.225	0.483	1.287	0.9515	1.0510	0.030	1.970	0.029	1.874	2.534	0.3946	0.848	0	5.079	0	2.004
7	1.134	0.419	1.182	0.9594	1.0424	0.118	1.882	0.113	1.806	2.704	0.3698	0.833	0.205	5.204	0.076	1.924
8	1.061	0.373	1.099	0.9650	1.0363	0.185	1.815	0.179	1.751	2.847	0.3512	0.820	0.388	5.307	0.136	1.864
9	1.000	0.337	1.032	0.9693	1.0317	0.239	1.761	0.232	1.707	2.970	0.3367	0.808	0.547	5.393	0.184	1.816
10	0.949	0.308	0.975	0.9727	1.0281	0.284	1.716	0.276	1.669	3.078	0.3249	0.797	0.686	5.469	0.223	1.777
11	0.905	0.285	0.927	0.9754	1.0253	0.321	1.679	0.313	1.637	3.173	0.3152	0.787	0.811	5.535	0.256	1.744
12	0.866	0.266	0.886	0.9776	1.0230	0.354	1.646	0.346	1.610	3.258	0.3069	0.778	0.923	5.594	0.283	1.717
13	0.832	0.249	0.850	0.9794	1.0210	0.382	1.618	0.374	1.585	3.336	0.2998	0.770	1.025	5.647	0.307	1.693
14	0.802	0.235	0.817	0.9810	1.0194	0.406	1.594	0.399	1.563	3.407	0.2935	0.763	1.118	5.696	0.328	1.672
15	0.775	0.223	0.789	0.9823	1.0180	0.428	1.572	0.421	1.544	3.472	0.2880	0.756	1.203	5.740	0.347	1.653
16	0.750	0.212	0.763	0.9835	1.0168	0.448	1.552	0.440	1.526	3.532	0.2831	0.750	1.282	5.782	0.363	1.637
17	0.728	0.203	0.739	0.9845	1.0157	0.466	1.534	0.458	1.511	3.588	0.2787	0.744	1.356	5.820	0.378	1.622
18	0.707	0.194	0.718	0.9854	1.0148	0.482	1.518	0.475	1.496	3.640	0.2747	0.739	1.424	5.856	0.391	1.609
19	0.688	0.187	0.698	0.9862	1.0140	0.497	1.503	0.490	1.483	3.689	0.2711	0.733	1.489	5.889	0.404	1.596
20	0.671	0.180	0.680	0.9869	1.0132	0.510	1.490	0.504	1.470	3.735	0.2677	0.729	1.549	5.921	0.415	1.585
21	0.655	0.173	0.663	0.9876	1.0126	0.523	1.477	0.516	1.459	3.778	0.2647	0.724	1.606	5.951	0.425	1.575
22	0.640	0.167	0.647	0.9882	1.0120	0.534	1.466	0.528	1.448	3.819	0.2618	0.720	1.660	5.979	0.435	1.565
23	0.626	0.162	0.633	0.9887	1.0114	0.545	1.455	0.539	1.438	3.858	0.2592	0.716	1.711	6.006	0.443	1.557
24	0.612	0.157	0.619	0.9892	1.0109	0.555	1.445	0.549	1.429	3.895	0.2567	0.712	1.759	6.032	0.452	1.548
25	0.600	0.135	0.606	0.9896	1.0105	0.565	1.435	0.559	1.420	3.931	0.2544	0.708	1.805	6.056	0.459	1.541

Glossary

3M's Waste Ratio: 3M calculates a simple "Waste ratio" to assess the environmental performance of their operations by the formula: (waste)/(waste + products + by products).

American National Standards Institute (ANSI): promotes the use of U.S. standards internationally, advocates U.S. policy and technical positions in international and regional standards organizations, and encourages the adoption of international standards as national standards where these meet the needs of the user community.

American Society for Quality (ASQ): assists in administering the Award Program under contract to NIST. ASQ is dedicated to the ongoing development, advancement, and promotion of quality concepts, principles, and techniques.

American Society for Testing Materials (ASTM): a not-for-profit organization that provides a forum for the development and publication of voluntary consensus standards for materials, products, systems, and services.

American Society of Mechanical Engineers (ASME): a nonprofit educational and technical organization created to promote and enhance the technical competency and activities in mechanical engineering.

Attribute Charts: used when the data being measured meet certain conditions or attributes. Attributes are involved in any situation where you have a quality characteristic that can be considered categorical (Griffin 2000).

Audit: the monitoring function conducted in an industrial organization to locate and report existing and potential hazards, or man-environment systems or conditions, that have the capacity to cause accidents or illnesses in the workplace.

Balanced Scorecard: a management system (not only a measurement system) that enables organizations to clarify their vision and strategy and translate them into action. It provides feedback around both the internal business processes and external outcomes in order to continuously improve strategic performance and results.

Bar Chart: a visual comparison of quantitative and categorical data; two or more series of data with multiple categories can be presented on the same chart for comparison purposes.

Behavior-Based Safety: a process designed to reduce the frequency of work-related accidents by first reducing the frequency of negative or inappropriate employee behaviors.

Benchmarking: the planned, deliberate process of seeking out and targeting competitive continuous improvement by emulating industry's "best practices."

Binomial Probability: a probability in which only two possible outcomes for an event are possible—such as a "heads/tails" or "yes/no" situation; the distribution of these probabilities is considered to be binomial.

Bivariate Correlations: a correlation with two variables, a dependent variable signified by the Y-axis and the independent variable signified by the X-axis. The independent variable influences the dependent variable.

Black Belt (BB): employees trained in Six Sigma whose main purpose is to lead quality projects and work full time until they are complete. Black Belts can typically complete four to six projects per year with savings of approximately $230,000 per project.

c-Chart: a chart used for "Poisson" processes. This type of chart, for example, can monitor the number of "events" in each of many equal samples (constant sample size). Occurrence reporting data (i.e.: number of accidents per month) empirically appear to fit the "Poisson" model.

CIPP Evaluation Model: an evaluation framework to serve managers and administrators facing four different kinds of educational decisions; context evaluation, input evaluation, process evaluation, and product evaluation.

Canada's National Quality Institute: a not-for-profit organization that provides strategic focus and direction for Canadian organizations to achieve excellence, enabling Canada to set the standard for quality and healthy workplace practices throughout the world.

Categorical Data: data that represents categories; also called discrete data. Categorical data with only two categories can be referred to as dichotomous data.

Cause and Effect Analysis: an analysis that is focused on attacking a problem rather than on fixing blame, useful in any kind of process capability analysis, not only as the result of attributes inspection and Pareto Analysis.

Combined Ratio: the expense ratio plus the loss ratio equals the "combined ratio."

Competitive Benchmarking: generally focuses on direct competitors within the same industry and with specific comparable business operations, or on indirect competitors in related industries (perhaps key customers or suppliers) having complementary business operations.

Compound Probabilities: the probability of the occurrence of multiple events in a situation. However, instead of determining the failure due to all events occurring at the same time, a person may wish to determine the occurrence of one or more event at a time.

Conditional Probabilities: a probability in which some condition or restriction is placed upon the sample that is being used to determine the probability.

Continuous Improvement Process: defining goals, measuring performance, and implementing follow-up action to improve performance.

Control Chart: a statistical device principally used for the study and control of repetitive processes. A control chart is a run chart with the addition of a line indicating the running average and two lines indicating the upper and lower control limits.

Correlation Procedures: used to indicate a measure of association between two or more variables.

Critical Behaviors: behaviors that have been identified as being critical to safety performance in the workplace. These behaviors can be identified using one of four different sources; incident reports, employee interviews, job observations and review of work rules and procedure manuals.

Cumulative Sum Trend Analysis Technique: a plot of the cumulative sequential differences between each data point and the process average over time. A positive slope of the graph indicates an average higher than the process average; a flat slope indicates an average the same as the process average; and a negative slope indicates an average less than the process average.

Current Indicators: indicators of how well the management systems are working at the present time.

Descriptive Statistics: statistical techniques that are used to describe the population or sample. Commonly used descriptive statistics include measures of central tendency; mean, median and mode and measures of variability; range, variance and standard deviation. Additional descriptive measures can include percentages, percentiles and frequencies.

DOE Cost Index: applies a weighting factor to the frequency of injury and illness cases. As a result, the index is approximately equal to cents lost per hour worked.

Economic Analysis: a traditional approach to analyis using the time value of money as the central concept. The time value of money is represented by discounting the cash flows produced by the investment to reflect the interest that would, in effect at least, have to be paid on the capital borrowed to finance the investment.

Environmental Accounting: a measurement of the environmental liabilities a firm faces due to its activities or an evaluation of the internal environmental costs for businesses.

Environmental Assessment of Sites and Organizations (EASO): an assessment that may be done during operations or at the time of acquisition or divesture of assets or may be conducted as part of a broader business assessment often referred to as 'due diligence'.

Environmental Auditing: evaluations of the procedures a firm uses to avoid environmental damages and to limit environmental liabilities.

European Foundation for Quality Management (EFQM): founded in 1988 by the Presidents of 14 major European companies, with the endorsement of the European Commission. The EFQM helps European businesses make better products and deliver improved services through the effective use of leading edge management practices.

European Quality Award: Europe's most prestigious Award for organizational excellence and the top level of the EFQM Levels of Excellence.

European Union's Eco-Management and Audit Scheme (EMAS): codified in the EU as the Eco-Management and Audit Regulation (EMAR). At this time, EMAR is a voluntary regulation for organizations in Europe, providing requirements for an EMS and environmental auditing program.

Expected Loss Ratio: a formula used by insurance companies to relate expected income to expected losses. The formula for the expected loss ratio is (expected incurred losses + expected loss adjusting expense) ÷ expected earned premiums.

Expense Ratios: costs to the insured in excess of the losses. Insurers must pay expenses such as special services like attorneys fees, rental fees, supplies and taxes all of which form a cost of doing business.

Experience Modification Rating (EMR): rating given to companies by the National Council on Compensation Insurance (NCCI) or other insurance rating groups. The rating system was established to provide all insureds with a level playing field, which protects both insurance companies and those whom they insure.

Expertise-Oriented Approach: the worth of a curriculum would be assessed by curriculum or subject-matter experts who would observe the curriculum in action, examine its content and underlying learning theory or, in some other way, glean sufficient information to render a considered judgment about its value.

Failure Modes and Effects Analysis: systems safety technique that analyzes systems' individual components for the purpose of identifying single point hazards.

Fault Tree Analysis: systems safety technique that utilizes a top down analysis approach, failure trees and Boolean logic.

Formative Evaluations: evaluations conducted during the operation of a program to provide program directors evaluative information useful in improving the program.

Functional Benchmarking: a comparison of performance and procedures between similar business functions, but in different organizations and industries.

Generic Benchmarking: benchmarking undertaken with external companies in different industries, which represent the 'best-in-class' for particular aspects of the selected business operations.

Genichi Taguchi: Japaneese engineer who developed a systematic approach for the application of experiments to improve product design and process quality.

Global Reporting Initiative (GRI): a long-term, multi-stakeholder, international undertaking whose mission is to develop and disseminate globally applicable sustainability reporting guidelines for voluntary use by organizations reporting on the economic, environmental, and social dimensions of their activities, products and services.

Green Belt (GB): employees trained in Six Sigma who spend a portion of their time completing projects, but maintain their regular work role and responsibilities. Depending on their workload, they can spend anywhere from 10% to 50% of their time on their project(s).

Histograms: charts that use continuous data and depict the obtained values on the continuous scale for each subject in the sample or population.

Incurred Losses: both losses paid out as benefits and administrative costs of processing these claims. The earned premium is that portion of the total charged to cover risk taken by the insurance company.

Insurance Loss Ratios: loss ratio, expense ratio, and combined ratio.

Internal Benchmarking: benchmarking done within an organization and typically between closely related divisions, similar plants or operations, or equivalent business units, using common or shared performance parameters as a basis for comparison to internal criteria only.

International Organization for Standardization: a non-governmental organization headquartered in Geneva, Switzerland. It is a federation of national standards bodies with a mission to promote the development of standardization and related activities in the world.

Interstate Experience Rating: a multi-state experience rating program developed by the National Council on Compensation Insurance for employers with multi-state operations. The experience of all the states is combined to determine the employer's experience modification.

Interval Data: a form of continuous data with zero as a placeholder on the scale.

ISO 9000: a set of international quality management system standards and guidelines. Since their initial publication in 1987, they have earned a global reputation as the basis for establishing quality management systems.

ISO 14000: Environmental Management Standards that provide a framework for businesses to voluntarily manage the environmental impact their products, processes and businesses have upon the environment.

ISO 9000:2000: involved in auditor certification or training, certification/registration of management systems, and accreditation or standardization in the area of conformity assessment.

Joint Event Probability: the probability of an event in which the researcher asks the question "What is the probability of event A and event B occurring at the same time?"

Leading Indicators: measures that can be effective in predicting future safety performance.

Life Cycle Assessment: environmental analyses used to examine environmental impacts along various points in the life cycle of the product, process, or activity.

Line Chart: charts used make comparisons of groups of continuous data. Each line represents a different group while the points on the lines represent the obtained values for each measurement period.

Loss Ratio: a formula used by insurers to relate loss expenses to income. Formula: (incurred losses + loss adjustment expenses) ÷ earned premiums.

Malcolm Baldrige National Quality Award: created by Public Law 100-107, signed into law on August 20, 1987. The award recognizes quality management systems.

Manual Premium: the premium developed by multiplying a published workers' compensation employee classification rate by each $100 of payroll for that employee classification.

Master Black Belt (MBB): employees trained in Six Sigma who work with the owners of the process to ensure that quality objectives and targets are set, plans are determined, progress is tracked, and education is provided. In the best Six Sigma organizations, process owners and MBBs work very closely and share information daily.

Measures of Central Tendency: statistics measures that describe how closely the data groups together. There are three measures of central tendency. They are the mean, median, and mode.

Measures of Variability: measures that indicate the spread of the data. The three measures of variability are the range, variance, and standard deviation.

MIL STD 882D: a military standard that specifically deals with system safety techniques and program requirements.

Modified Premium: the manual premium developed for an employer multiplied by the employer's experience modification.

np-Charts: charts used to analyze nonconforming items over a constant area of opportunity and with constant sample sizes.

National Fire Protection Association: international nonprofit organization with a mission to reduce the worldwide burden of fire and other hazards on the quality of life by providing and advocating scientifically based consensus codes and standards, research, training and education.

Normal Distribution: a hypothetical distribution that would be expected when completely random, continuous data is collected from a population. The normal distribution is commonly referred to as the "bell-shaped" curve because of its noted shape, which resembles the outline of a bell.

North American Industry Classification System (NAICS): replaces the U.S. Standard Industrial Classification (SIC) system. NAICS is the first-ever North American industry classification system. The U.S., Canada, and Mexico developed the system to provide comparable statistics across the three countries.

Ordinal Data: rank order data. Ordinal means order, and ordinal data allows the researcher to order the data in some fashion.

OSHA-Based Incidence Rates: one of the more common methods of measuring safety performance, including OSHA recordable injury incidence rates, recordable illness incidence rates, death rates, and lost day case injury rates.

OSHA's Gravity-Based Penalty System: establishes the initial penalty based on the potential severity of loss that the hazard poses and the probability that an injury or illness could occur because of the alleged violation.

OSHA's VPP Program: program designed to recognize and promote effective safety and health management.

p-Chart: a chart used with "binomial" data. P-charts are used for results of go-no go tests.

P-D-C-A Cycle: Plan-Do-Check-Act management process that underlies the continual improvement process.

Pareto Analysis: is used to identify and evaluate types of nonconformities. The Pareto Diagram will direct attention to the most frequent nonconformities but not necessarily to the most important.

Pareto Principle: states that in any population that contributes to a common effect, a relative few of the contributors – the vital few – account for the bulk of the effect.

Pearson Correlation Procedure: is used when both variables are continuous in nature.

Penalty Factors: factors used to reduce the penalty from the initial gravity-based penalty level. The three factors are the size of the business, the good faith of the employer, and the employer's history of previous violations.

Perception Surveys: surveys used to measure attitudes toward, and acceptance of, safety and health programs.

Performance Indexing: requires the results of the audit to be quantified in a manner that allows for comparisons against performance benchmarks.

Performance Measures: indicators that focus on gaps or other factors that can affect a site's safety and business success.

Pie Chart: a chart in which each component of the series (of quantitative or qualitative data) is represented by a wedge (piece of pie) proportional to its frequency in the series.

Poisson Probability: the probability of an event if the frequency of occurrence of the event is quite low compared to the overall exposure.

Procedure Analysis: technique used to examine the steps in a procedure or task for the purpose of identifying hazards and developing prevention strategies.

Process Capability: the measured, inherent reproducibility of the product turned out by the process. Inherent reproducibility refers to the uniformity resulting from a process that is in a state of statistical control.

Program Logic Model: a model describing the course of action a program takes to achieve its vision and strategic goals, often used in a setting in which program staff, partners, and customers collaborate.

QS-9000: shorthand name for "Quality System Requirements QS-9000." It is the common supplier quality standard for Chrysler Corporation, Ford Motor Company, and General Motors Corporation.

r-Chart: a control chart that plots the ranges of the samples. The range of the sample is the difference between the largest observation and the smallest.

Range: the difference between the lowest value and the highest value data points.

Ratio Data: continuous data that does not have zero as an arbitrary placeholder on the scale. Zero on this scale represents absence of the characteristic.

Ratio of Lost Workdays to Lost Workday Cases: a severity measure for injuries and illnesses.

Regression: procedures that allow a person to develop a prediction equation that can be used to predict dependent variables from independent variables.

Responsible Care: an obligation of membership in the American Chemistry Council that requires member companies to continually improve their health, safety, and environmental performance; listen and respond to public concerns; and assist each other to achieve optimum performance.

Root Cause Analysis: analysis that identifies causal factors relating to a mishap or near-miss incidents.

Run Chart: a preliminary display of the performance indicator data. It is simply the raw data for each time interval plotted on a chart. Average and control limits have not yet been added.

s-Chart: an x-chart with the sample standard deviation, s, used in place of the sample range to measure the process dispersion.

Safety Goals: are more long range than objectives and they may or may not be quantitatively measurable

Safety Metrics: the body of knowledge used to quantify and measure safety performance.

Safety Metrics Program: the process of systematically gathering data and analyzing it in an attempt to determine whether the organization's performance goals have been met.

Safety Objectives: cover a shorter term and are always measurable.

Scatterplots: a graph containing a cluster of dots that represents all pairs of observations. Each point on a scatterplot represents one case.

Simple Event Probabilities: probabilities in which the researcher compares the number of times an event occurred to the total number of possible outcomes.

Six Sigma: a highly structured program for improving business processes.

Society of Automotive Engineers: a society consisting of over 83,000 engineers, business executives, educators, and students that serves as a network, shares information, and exchanges ideas for advancing the engineering of mobility systems.

Standard Deviation: the square of the average difference from the mean for the scores in a distribution.

Standard Industrial Classification Manual: contains the Standard Industrial Classification which is used to classify establishments by type of activity in which they are engaged.

Summative Evaluation: an evaluation conducted at the end of the program to provide potential consumers with judgments about the programs worth or merit.

Total Quality Management: a management philosophy focusing on perpetual process enhancement, through the prevention of problems and errors; continual monitoring and control of processes, performance, and quality; the placing of the customer at the hub of attention; as well as a sense of awareness, commitment, and involvement on the part of management, all the workers, the customers, and suppliers.

Toxic Release Inventory: raw flux measurement system; mandated by the 1986 Emergency Planning and Community Right-to-Know Act.

Trailing Indicators: the traditional metrics that measure past safety efforts.

Trending and Forecasting: techniques used for detecting past patterns and projecting them into the future.

Tylerian Evaluation Approach: a process by which one determines the extent to which the educational objectives of a curriculum are being achieved.

u-Chart: a chart used to count "defects" per sample when the sample size varies for each "inspection".

UCLA Evaluation Model: as defined by UCLA—"the process of ascertaining the decision areas of concern, selecting appropriate information, and collecting and analyzing information in order to report summary data useful to decision-makers in selecting among alternatives."

Underwriting Expenses: costs of writing a policy, sales commissions, salaries, office space, etc. The written premium is that portion of the total premium charged to cover these expenses. Typically, the written premium is about 30 percent of the total; the remaining 70 percent covers claims—both legitimate and fraudulent—made against the insurance company.

Variance: a measure of how much the individual data points vary from the distribution mean. The variance is the average of the squared deviations from the mean.

W. Edwards Deming: an American statistician, educator, and consultant whose advocacy of quality-control methods in industrial production aided Japan's economic recovery after World War II and its subsequent rise to global supremacy in many industries in the late 20th century.

x-Chart: a chart used primarily with "variable" data, which are usually measurements such as the length of an object, the time it takes to complete a process, or the number of objects produced per period.

References

Aallan, C.; J. Sommerville; P. Kennedy; H. Robertson. 2000. Driving for business excellence through environmental performance improvements. *Total Quality Management,* 11(4–6):602–8.

Adams, Shawn. Benchmarks of safety quality. *Professional Safety.* 42(11):33–35.

Aldred, Katherine. 'Baldrige Index' outperforms S&P 500. *IIE Solutions.* 30(4):9.

Alkin, M.C. Evaluation theory development. *Evaluation Comment.* 2(2):2–7.

American Chemistry Council. *Responsible care. 2001.* Web citation: www.cmahq.com.

American National Standards Institute. 2001. Web citation: www.ansi.org.

American Psychological Association. 1995. *Publication manual.* 4th ed. Washington. D.C.: American Psychological Association.

American Society for Mechanical Engineers. 2002. Web citation: www.asme.org.

American Society for Quality. 2001. Web citation: www.asq.org.

———. 2001. *Certified six sigma black belt.* American Society for Quality.

American Society for Testing and Materials International. *ASTM annual report: 2000.* West Conshohocken, PA: ASTM International.

Anastasi, Anne. 1988. *Psychological testing.* New York: Macmillian Publishing Company.

Balanced Scorecard Institute. 2001. *The Balanced Scorecard Institute.* Website Citation: www.balancedscorecard.org.

Bennett, Martin and Peter James. ISO 14031 and the future of environmental performance evaluation. *Greener Management International.* Spring 98 (21):71–86.

Bickelhaupt, David. 1983. *General insurance.* Homewood, IL: Richard D. Irwin.

Bissell, A. F. 1990. Control charts and cusums for high precision processes. *Total Quality Management.* 1(2):221–29.

———. 1988. Cusum charts—give your data a new look. *International Journal of Quality & Reliability Management.* Vol. 5, no. 2. Black, S.A. and H.C. Crumley. Self-assessment: What's in it for us? *Total Quality Management.* 8(2/3); S90, 4p

Bok, Ann and George Shields. *Rising expense ratios, analysis of rising expense ratios.* Website citation: www.ncci.com.

Bonnie, Richard J. 1999. *Reducing the burden of injury.* Washington, D.C.: National Academy Press.

Bowles, Jerry and Joshua Hammond. Quality is not enough. *Corporate Board.* 12(71):19.

Bruce, Susan M. and Tom T. Hwang. Web-based teacher preparation in visual impairment. *Journal of Visual Impairment & Blindness.* 95(10):609–23.

Burke, W. Warner and William Trahant. 2000. *Business climate shifts.* Woburn, MA: Butterworth-Heinemann.

Caulcutt, Roland. Why is Six Sigma so successful? *Journal of Applied Statistics.* 28(3/4):301–7.

Christine, Brian. Benchmarking to improve fleet safety. *Risk Management.* 41(2):57–58.

Conti, Tito. Vision 2000: Positioning the new ISO 9000 standards with respect to total quality management models. *Total Quality Management.* 10(4/5):S454–465.

Czarnecki, Mark T. 1999. *Managing by measuring.* Chicago: American Management Association.

Daugherty, Jack E. 1999. *Industrial safety management.* Rockville, MD: Government Institutes.

Deming, W. Edwards. 2000. *Out of the crisis.* Boston, MA: MIT Press.

DeVito, Denise and Sara Morrison. Benchmarking: A tool for sharing and cooperation. *Journal for Quality & Participation.* 23(4):56–62.

Duncan, Acheson. 1974. *Quality control and industrial statistics.* Richard D. Irwin, Homewood, IL.

Dupont Corporation. 2001. *Executive Safety News.* Website citation: www.dupont.com/safety/esnmenu.html.

Eckes, George. 2001. *The Six Sigma Revolution.* New York, NY: John Wiley and Sons.

Emery, Robert and Susanne M. Savely. Soliciting employee concerns during routine safety inspections. *Professional Safety.* 42(7):36–39.

Encyclopedia Britannica, 2000.

European Union. Web Citation: europa.eu.int/comm/environment/emas/intro_en.htm#What%20is%20EMAS?

European Foundation for Quality Management Levels of Excellence. 2001. *European quality award information brochure.* Brussels, Belgium.

———. 2001. Website citation: www.efqm.org.

———. 1999. *Eight essentials of excellence—the fundamental concepts and their benefits.* Brussels, Belgium.

Farnum, Nicholas. 1993. *Modern statistical quality control and improvement.* Brooks/Cole Pub Corp.

Gage, N.L. and David C. Berliner. 1988. *Educational psychology*. Gevena, IL: Houghton Mifflin Company.

Garner, Charlotte A. and Patricia O. Horn. How smart managers improve safety and health systems. *Professional Safety*. 45(6):28–32.

Geller, E. Scott . Behavior based safety. *Occupational Health and Safety*. January 1999:40–49.

Global Reporting Initiative. 2000. *GRI and the sustainability reporting guidelines*. Boston, MA.

Griffin, Gary. 2000. *The quality technician's handbook*. Upper Saddle River, NJ: Prentice Hall. 439–440.

Hansen, Larry, Rate your "B.O.S.S."—Benchmarking organizational safety strategy. *Professional Safety*. 39(6):37–43.

Hays, William. 1988. *Statistics*. Orlando: Holt, Rinehart, and Winston.

Hidley, John H. Critical success factors for behavior based safety. *Professional Safety*. 43(7):30–35.

Hodgetts, Richard M. 1998. *Measures of quality and high performance*. New York, NY: AMACOM.

Holloway, Jacky; Jenny Lewis; and Geoff Mallory. 1995. *Performance measurement and evaluation*. Thousands Oaks, CA: Sage Publications.

Horvath, Theodore. 1974. *Basic statistics for the behavioral sciences*. Glenview, IL: Scott, Foresman and Company.

Huyink, David and Craig Westover. 1994. *ISO 9000: motivating people, mastering the process, achieving registration*. Chicago, IL: Richard D. Irwin.

IIE Solutions. More employers conducting safety self-audits. 31(12):12.

———. Baldrige Award winners do better. 33(6):16.

International Organization for Standardization. 2001. *ISO directory of ISO 9000 and ISO 14000 accreditation and certification bodies*. Web citation: www.iso.ch/iso/en/PDFs/accr_bodies_dir.rtf

———. 2001. *The ISO survey of ISO 9000 and ISO 14000 certificates tenth cycle*. Geneva Switzerland.

———. 2001. *Technical committee 176 on quality management and quality assurance*. Web citation: www.tc176.org.

———. 2001. *Technical committee 207: environmental management*. Web citation: www.tc207.org.

———. 2001. Web Citation: www.iso.ch/iso/en/iso9000-14000/tour/plain.html

———. 2000. *ISO bulletin*. Geneva, Switzerland.

———. 1998. *ISO 14000: Meet the whole family*. Geneva, Switzerland.

————. 1998. *Publicizing your ISO 9000 or ISO 14000 certification.* Geneva, Switzerland.

Ishikawa, Kaoru. 1982. *Guide to quality control.* Tokyo, Japan: Asian Productivity Organization.

Janicak, Christopher. 2000. *Applied statistics in occupational safety and health.* Rockville, MD: Government Institutes.

Johnson, Gregory. 1997. *The ISO 14000 EMS audit handbook.* Boca Raton, FL: St. Lucie Press.

Johnson, Linda F. Benchmarks for successful training. *Occupational Health and Safety.* 68(8):104–106.

Johnson, Perry. 1993. *ISO 9000: Meeting the new international standards.* New York, NY: McGraw Hill.

Juran, Joseph and Godfrey Blanton. 1999. *Juran's quality handbook.* New York, NY: McGraw Hill.

Kaufman, Roger; Sivasailam Thiagarajan; and Paula MacGillis. 1997. *The guidebook for performance improvement.* San Francisco, CA: Jossey-Bass, Pfeiffer.

Kirkpatrick, D. L. 1987. Evaluation of training. In *Training and development handbook.* 3rd ed. Edited by R. L. Craig. New York, NY: McGraw-Hill. 301–319.

Krause, Thomas R. Moving to the 2nd Generation In Behavior Based Safety. *Professional Safety.* 46(5):27–32.

Krause, Thomas R. and John H. Hidley. 1990. *The behavior based safety process.* New York, NY: Van Nostrand Reinhold.

Kuzma, Jan. 1992. *Basic statistics for the health sciences.* Mountain View, CA: Mayfield Publishing Company.

Landesberg, Phil. In the beginning, there were Deming and Juran. *Journal for Quality & Participation.* 22(6):59–62.

Lanen, William N. Waste minimization at 3M company. *Journal of Management Accounting Research.* 11:29, 15p

Leandri, Susan J. Measures that matter: how to fine-tune your performance measures. *Journal for Quality & Participation.* 24(1):39–41.

Lippert, Robert M.; Rama Radhakrishna; Owen Plank; and Charles C. Mitchell. Using different evaluation tools to assess a regional internet inservice training. *International Journal of Instructional Media.* 28(3):237–49.

Lokkegaard, Kristian. ISO 14031 used as a tool in ISO 14001 or as an alternative for a simple EMS. *Greener Management International.* no. 28: 79–90.

The Malcolm Baldrige National Quality Improvement Act of 1987. Public Law 107. 100th Cong., 1st sess., 6 January 1987.

Manuele, Fred A. Principles of the practice of safety. *Professional Safety.* July 1997. 27–31.

Martin, Jay G . and Gerald J. Edgley. 1998. *Environmental management systems.* Rockville, MD: Government Institutes.

Matthews, Jan M. and Alan M. Hudson. Guidelines for evaluating parent training programs. *Family Relations.* 50(1):77–87.

National Fire Protection Association. 2002. Web Citation: www.nfpa.org

National Institute of Standards and Technology. 2001. *Baldrige National Quality Program.* Web Citation: www.quality.nist.gov/Improvement_Act.htm.

———. 2001. *Baldrige National Quality Program, 2001 Criteria for Performance Excellence.* Gaithersburg, MD: United States Department of Commerce. Baldrige National Quality Program.

National Quality Institute. 2001. *Canada Awards for Excellence Entry Guide.* Toronto, Ontario: National Quality Institute.

———. 2001. Toronto, Ontario. Web citation: www.nqi.ca/english/

National Safety Council. 1997. *Accident Prevention Manual for Business and Industry; Administration and Programs.* Itasca, IL: National Safety Council.

Oluoch-Wauna, Lucas O. 2001. *EMAS and ISO 14001.* Environmental Policy and Law 31/4-5.

Pearch, Clyde and Jill Kitka. ISO 9000: 2000—the new international standard for quality. *Power Engineering.* 104(8):56–59.

Petersen, Dan. Safety management 2000: Our strengths & weaknesses. *Professional Safety.* 45(1):16–19.

———. What Measures should we use, and why? *Professional Safety.* 43(10):37–41.

Phillips, Jack J. 1991. *Handbook of training evaluation and measurement methods.* Houston, TX: Gulf Publishing Company.

Pierce, F. David. Setting effective goals and objectives in safety and health programs, *Occupational Hazards.* 57(10):169–174.

———. *Total quality for safety professionals.* Rockville, MD: Government Institutes.

Poll, Roswitha. Performance, processes and costs: Managing service quality with the balanced scorecard. *Library Trends.* 49(4):709.

Pyzdek, Thomas. 2001. *The six sigma handbook.* New York, NY: McGraw Hill Publishing.

Quality America Incorporated. 2001. *Cusum control limits.* Web Citation: www.qualityamerica.com.

Robotham, George. Safety training that works. *Professional Safety.* 46(5):33–38.

Rouse, William B. Factors of the experience modification rating and why they mean. *Professional Safety.* 42(9):27–29.

Rouse, William B and Kenneth R. Boff. Making the case for investments in human effectiveness. *Information, Knowledge & Systems Management.* 1(3/4):225–48.

Rupp, Richard V. 1991. *Rupp's insurance and Risk management glossary.* Web Citation: www.nits.com/rupps/

Sabroski, Suzanne. NAICS codes: A new classification system for a new economy. *Searcher.* 8(10):18–25.

Schofield, J.W. and K.M. Anderson. 1984. *Combining quantitative and qualitative methods in research on ethnic identity and intergroup relations.* Paper presented at the Society for Research on Child Development Study Group on Ethnic Socialization. Los Angeles.

Schulze, Peter C. *Measures of environmental performance and ecosystem condition.* 1999. Washington, D.C.: National Academy Press.

Scriven, M. 1967. The methodology of evaluation. In R.E. Statke, Curriculum Evaluation. *American Educational Research Association Monograph Series on Evaluation.* Chicago: Rand McNally. No. 1.

Shand, Dawne. Six sigma. *Computerworld.* 35(10):38.

Shlomo, Waks and Frank Moti. Principles and the ISO 9000 standards in engineering education. *European Journal of Engineering Education.* 24(3):249–59.

Simmons, Michael. Leadership. *Total quality management.* 8(2/3):273–75.

Society of Automotive Engineers. Web citation: www.sae.org.

Stephenson, Joe. 1991. *System safety 2000.* New York, NY: Van Nostrand Reinhold.

Stricoff, R. Scott. Safety performance measurement. *Professional Safety.* 45(1):36–40.

Stufflebeam, D.L. The relevance of the CIPP Evaluation model for educational accountability. *Journal of Research and Development in Education.* 5(1):19–25.

Systems Safety Society. 1997. *System safety analysis handbook.* Systems Safety Society.

Taggart, Michael D. and Horlin Carter Sr. Assessment matrices for benchmarking EH&S programs. *Professional Safety.* 44(5):34–38.

Tibor, Tom and Ira Feldman. 1997. *Implementing ISO 14000.* Chicago, IL: Irwin Publishing.

Tiller, Blinn, Kelly and Head. 1989. *Essential of risk financing, volume #1.* Amlvern, PA: Insurance Institute of America.

Training Resources and Data Exchange (TRADE) Performance-Based Management Special Interest Group (PBM SIG). 1995. *How to measure performance—a handbook of techniques and tools.*

United States Census Bureau. 2001. *North American industry classification system (NAICS).* Web citation: www.census.gov/epcd/www/naics.html.

United States Department of Defense. 1984. *MIL-STD-882B system safety program requirements.* Washington, D.C.: Department of Defense.

———. 2000. *MIL-STD-882D system safety program requirements.* Washington, D.C.: Department of Defense.

United States Department of Energy, Hanford Site. 2001. *Implementing performance measures.* Web citation: www.hanford.gov/safety/vpp/busobj2.htm.

———. 2001. *Generating and using control charts.* Web citation: www.hanford.gov/safety/vpp/spc.htm.

United States Department of Energy, Office of Environment, Safety, and Health. 2001. *Occupational injury and property damage summary.* Web citation: tis.eh.doe.gov/docs/oipds/archive/4_94/inj_ill.html.

United States Department of Labor, Bureau of Labor Statistics. 1997. *Census of fatal occupational injuries.* Washington, D.C.: U.S. Government Printing Office.

———. 1997. *Handbook of methods.* Washington, D.C.: U.S. Government Printing Office.

United States Department of Labor, Occupational Safety and Health Administration. 2001. *Field Inspection Reference Manual.* Washington, D.C.

———. 1996. *OSHA directives: TED 8.1a—revised voluntary protection programs (VPP) policies and procedures manual.* Washington, D.C.

United States Environmental Protection Agency. 1995. *An introduction to environmental accounting as a business management tool.* Washington, D.C.: Office of Pollution Prevention and Toxics. Document #742-R-95-001.

———. 1995. *Federal Facility Pollution Prevention Project Analysis.* Washington, D.C.

———. *Measuring Environmental Performance.* Web citation: www.epa.gov/emergingstrategies/account.html.

United States Office of Management and Budget. 1987. *Standard Industrial Classification Manual.* Washington, D.C.: U.S. Government Printing Office.

van Houten, Gerry. ISO 9001:2000. *Information Management Journal.* 34(2):28–36.

Videras, Julio and Anna Alberini. The appeal of voluntary appeal of voluntary environmental programs. *Contemporary Economic Policy.* 18(4):449–462.

Vokurka, Robert J. The Baldrige at 14. *Journal for Quality & Participation.* 24(2):13–20.

Von Zharen, W.M. 1996. *ISO 14000: Understanding the environmental standards.* Rockville, MD: Government Institutes.

Waks, Shlomo and Moti Frank. 1999. Application of the total quality management approach principles and the ISO 9000 standards in engineering education. *European Journal of Engineering Education.* 24(3):249.

Waxer, Charles. 2001. *Six sigma organizational architecture.* iSixSigma. Website citation: www.isixsigma.com.

Weinstein, Michael B. Improving behavior based safety through TQM. *Professional Safety.* 43(1):29–34.

Weirauch, Wendy. EMS to acquire ISO standards. *Hydrocarbon Processing.* 74(9):33.

Westlund, Anders H. Measuring environmental impact on society in the EFQM system.

Total Quality Management. 12(1):125–136.

Wexley, K.N. and G.P. Latham. 1981. *Developing and training human resources in organizations.* Glenview, IL: Scott, Foresman, and Company.

Willig, John T. 1994. *Environmental TQM.* Chicago, IL: McGraw-Hill.

Witte, Robert and John Witte. 1997. *Statistics.* New York, NY: Harcourt Brace College Publishers.

Worthen, Blaine R. and James Sanders. 1987. *Educational evaluation.* New York, NY: Longman.

Solutions to

Chapter Questions

Chapter I

1. Provide examples of three different measures that are commonly used to measure safety performance:

    Number of work injuries, number of lost workdays, financial losses.

2. Historically, how well have the performance measures safety professionals selected measured performance?

    Historically, practitioners have chosen ineffective, inadequate, and invalid measures.

3. What is safety metrics?

    Safety metrics is the group of business practices and statistical procedures that is used to implement a process of measuring safety programs for determining acceptable levels of performance.

4. What is a safety metrics program?

    A safety metrics program includes the activities of program development, benchmarking, auditing, measuring performance, evaluating outcomes, and managing the program based upon the outcomes.

5. Describe the safety metrics process:

    A safety metrics program requires the process of systematically gathering data and analyzing it in an attempt to determine whether the organization's performance goals have been met.

6. What is the underlying premise of a safety metrics program?

    An underlying premise for safety metrics is that of continual performance improvement.

7. Define performance measures:

    Performance measures are indicators that focus on gaps and other factors that can affect a site's safety and business success.

8. An approach to quantifying performance measures should include what?

    The quantification of performance should be done through a systematic approach involving:

    a. Definition of standardized units of measure.

    b. Development of instruments and methods that are capable of measuring in terms of the units of measure

    c. Use of the instruments or methods to quantify performance

9. What purpose does data analysis and statistics serve with regards to measuring safety performance?

    Descriptive and inferential statistics can be used to assess safety data with a degree of statistical significance, thus providing a level of certainty to the results.

10. Describe the current trends in use for measuring safety performance in the work-place:

    Today's safety professional has moved beyond the standard measurement of safety performance in terms of the number of accidents or injuries and recordable injury and illness rates. Examples of performance measures include safe behaviors, program implementation, compliance, etc.

Chapter 2

1. Define performance measures:

    Performance measures are quantitative measures about an organizational aspect that provide an indication of the status of what is being measured.

2. What importance do performance measures have for an organization with regards to safety?

    Performance measures can be assessed using safety metrics for determining the status of a safety program.

3. What type of process should one follow when developing performance measures?

    Establish a team to develop the performance measures. Determine the organizational needs. Identify measures that will determine the status of where the organization is relative to those needs. Measure the status, then determine follow up action.

4. Describe a methodology for implementing performance measures in the work-place:

    One example of a methodology is 1) Mission and Vision; 2) Safety Objectives; and 3) Performance Measures.

5. Define key objectives, outcome measures, and activity measures:

Key objectives are those goals that articulate what a company expects from a business process. Outcome measures reflect the company's key objectives and are used to determine whether the company has reached them. Activity measures monitor the performance of activities that are instrumental in reaching the key objectives.

6. Differentiate between qualitative measures and quantitative measures:

Qualitative performance measurements, such as checklists, are commonly used to assess the status of safety and health programs. Quantitative, or objective, performance measurements are necessary for precision, consistency, and reproducibility.

7. Describe three benefits of performance measures:

Examples of benefits include:

- *Measures are flexible and allow for individual supervisory styles.*
- *The same measure need not be used for all supervisors.*
- *They are excellent for use in objective-setting approaches.*
- *They measure the presence, rather than the absence, of safety.*

Chapter 3

1. Define the measures of central tendency and the measures of variability:

Central tendency: mean, median, and mode

Variability: range, variance, standard deviation

2. The following data was collected from CJD Industries over a 12 month period:

Month	Number of Injuries
January	5
February	8
March	9
April	5
May	4
June	6
July	7
August	4
September	8
October	9
November	5
December	4

Calculate the mean, median, mode, standard deviation, range, and variance for the number of injuries that occurred per month.

Mean: 6.17

Median: 5.5

Mode: 4 and 5

Range: 5

Variance: 3.79

Standard Deviation: 1.95

3. Differentiate between ordinal, nominal, ratio and interval data formats:

Ordinal: rank data

Nominal: categorical data

Interval data: zero exists as a place holder (temperature)

Ratio data: zero represents absence of the characteristic (ie: weight)

4. What percentage of the population would expect to fall between the mean and two standard deviations?

47.72%

5. If it was determined that the probability of a system failure due to component A is .0003 and the probability of a system failure due to component B is .0001, what is the probability of a system failure due to A and B?

3×10^{-8}

6. If it was determined that the probability of a system failure due to component A is .0002 and the probability of a system failure due to component B is .0004, what is the probability of a system failure due to A or B assuming A and B could occur at the same time?

6.0×10^{-4}

7. It was determined that the probability of having one accident during a five-day workweek was .003. What is the probability of having exactly 3 accidents in a five-day work week?

2.7×10^{-7}

8. What are the probability formulas for a joint event, compound event, and simple event probability?

Joint Event = P(A or B) = P(A) + P(B) − P(A X B)

Compound Event = P(A and B) = P(A) × P(B)

Simple Event = P(A) = Number of Wanted Events/Total number of possible events

9. What is the maximum value a probability can have?

1.00

10. Describe the impact data representing a sample versus a population has upon calculating a variance and standard deviation:

    When calculating the variance and the standard deviation, if the data represents a sample, the denominator in the variance is equal to "N − 1." When calculating the variance and the standard deviation, if the data represents a population, the denominator in the variance is equal to "N."

Chapter 4

1. Differentiate between a run chart and a control chart:

   A control chart is a run chart with the addition of a line indicating the running average and two lines indicating the upper and lower control limits. A run chart is the raw data for each time interval plotted on a chart.

2. Define the following: x-axis, y-axis, UCL, LCL:

   The x-axis on a control chart identifies the time in which the measurement was taken. The y-axis on a control chart indicates the value of that measurement. The UCL is the upper control limit and the LCL is the lower control limit. Points located outside these limits are consider to be out of control.

3. What is a "run down of 6" mean for a control chart?

   A run down of 6 indicates that there are 6 points in succession that are trending downward at a significant rate.

4. What does it mean when a control chart is "out of control?"

   A chart is considered out of control when data indicates trends in data over time that need to be addressed because they fall outside of the acceptable ranges.

5. If there is a significant change identified on a control chart, what action can be taken?

   Examples include constructing a new control chart with the average control limits or addressing the reasons for the changes, which means evaluating the program to identify the reasons for the changes.

6. Describe the uses for p, u, c, and np charts:
   - *p-chart, for controlling the number of nonconforming items.*
   - *u-chart, for controlling the number of nonconformities per item.*
   - *c-chart, for controlling the number of nonconformities.*
   - *np- chart, for controlling the number of nonconformities.*

7. Describe the uses for r, x and s charts:

   These control charts are referred to as variable control charts. They are based upon measurements of quality characteristics.

8. What is a common number of standard deviations used to signify upper and lower control limits?

    3 standard deviations is common level for upper and lower control limits.

9. The following data was obtained from CJD Industries. Develop an "s chart" for the data.

n	Instrument Reading #1	Instrument Reading #2	Instrument Reading # 3
1	1.7	1.6	1.9
2	1.8	1.7	1.2
3	1.9	1.8	1.3
4	1.2	1.9	1.4
5	1.4	1.2	1.7
6	1.5	1.3	1.8
7	1.8	1.4	1.2
8	1.9	1.5	1.3
9	2	1.1	1.4
10	2.1	1.4	1.5

The upper and lower control limits for an s chart are calculated as follows:

$$\overline{S} = .31$$

$$UCL = B(4) \times \overline{S} = 2.568 \times .31 = .80$$

$$LCL = B(3) \times \overline{S} = 0 \times .31 = 0$$

The standard deviations and average appear in the following table:

n	Instrument Reading #1	Instrument Reading #2	Instrument Reading # 3	*Standard Deviation*
1	1.7	1.6	1.9	*0.15*
2	1.8	1.7	1.2	*0.32*
3	1.9	1.8	1.3	*0.32*
4	1.2	1.9	1.4	*0.36*
5	1.4	1.2	1.7	*0.25*
6	1.5	1.3	1.8	*0.25*
7	1.8	1.4	1.2	*0.31*
8	1.9	1.5	1.3	*0.31*
9	2	1.1	1.4	*0.46*
10	2.1	1.4	1.5	*0.38*
Average				*0.31*

The completed chart is as follows:

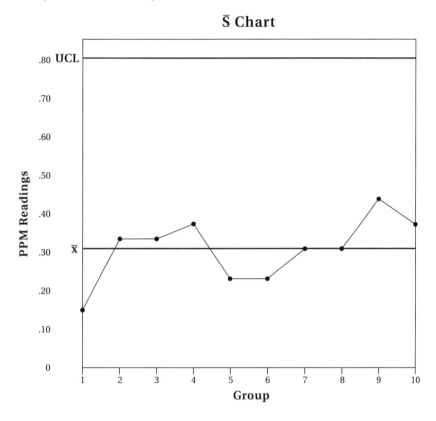

S̄ Chart

10. What is a Pareto Diagram and Pareto Analysis used to identify?

Pareto Analysis is used to identify and evaluate types of nonconformities. The Pareto Diagram will direct attention to the most frequent nonconformities but not necessarily to the most important.

Chapter 5

1. What does a correlation indicate?

A correlation indicates the degree to which a relationship exists between variables.

2. What is a bivariate correlation?

A bivariate correlation is a correlation between two variables.

3. Draw a scatterplot that would be indicative of a strong positive correlation:

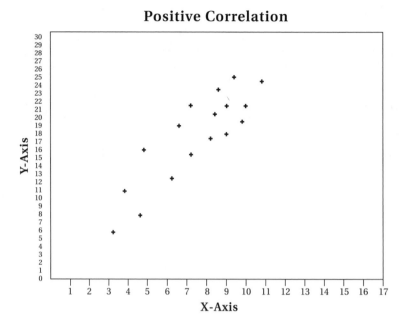

4. The following data was obtained from Company CJT. What is the Pearson correlation coefficient:

Case	Fire Losses (Y)	Y²	Minutes for Fire Brigade to Respond (X)	X²	XY
1	$100	$10000	15	225	$1500
2	$200	$40000	26	676	$5200
3	$250	$62500	54	2916	$13500
4	$500	$250000	40	1600	$20000
5	$200	$40000	18	324	$3600
Sum	$1250	$402500	153	5741	$43800
Std Dev	$150		16.27		
Average	$250		30.6		

Pearson Correlation Coefficient = .57

5. A correlation procedure yielded a correlation coefficient of .89. What is the coefficient of determination and what does it represent?

    .89 × .89 = .79. 79% of the variability in Y can be explained by the variability in X.

6. What can a regression procedure be used for?

    Regression procedures can be used to predict a dependent variable from an independent one.

7. If a correlation equation yielded a correlation coefficient of .89 and the standard deviation of X was .18 and the standard deviation of Y was .34. The average for X is 3.0 and the average for Y is 3.7. What is the equation of the line?

   $Y = 1.68(X) + (-1.34)$

8. Using the information in Item 7, what would one expect for a value on Y if a value of 6 was obtained for the X variable?

   $Y = 1.68(6) + (-1.34) = 8.74$

9. How is trending and forecasting used in a safety performance program?

   Trending and forecasting can be used to predict future performance based upon past safety performance.

10. What are the data requirements for the Pearson Correlation Procedure?

    In order to use the Pearson Correlation Coefficient, two variables that are continuous in nature are required. The variables should be in the ratio or interval format.

Chapter 6

1. What is a scatterpot used to represent?

   A scatterplot is a graph containing a cluster of dots that represents all pairs of observations

2. What is the difference between the variable plotted along the horizontal axis versus the vertical axis on a scatterplot?

   On a scatterplot, the independent variable is plotted along the horizontal axis (X) and the dependent variable along the vertical (Y) axis.

3. The following data was collected from Company CJD. Develop a histogram that represents the data:

Subject	Measurement
1	50
2	51
3	50
4	49
5	48
6	50
7	51
8	50
9	49
10	50
11	51
12	48
13	50
14	50
15	51
16	50
17	49
18	50
19	51
20	48

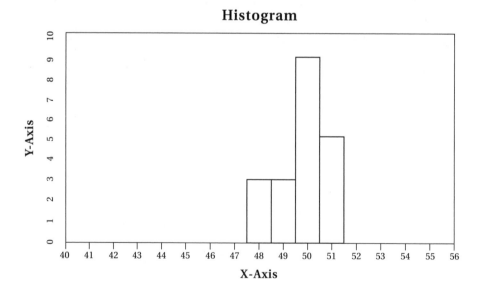

4. The following data was collected from Company CJD. Develop a line chart that represents the data:

Time	Group #1	Group #2	Group #3
8:00 a.m.	3	2	2
9:00 a.m.	2	3	3
10:00 a.m.	3	3	3
11:00 a.m.	5	1	1
12:00 a.m.	4	4	4
1:00 p.m.	2	4	4
2:00 p.m.	1	5	5
3:00 p.m.	5	4	4
4:00 p.m.	4	2	2
5:00 p.m.	5	2	2

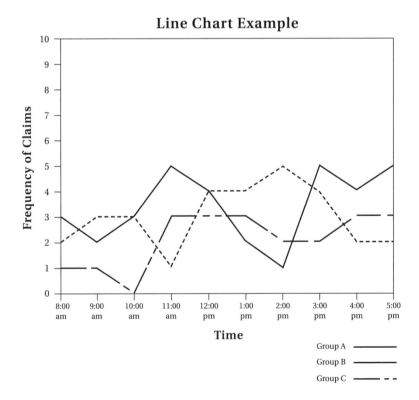

5. The following data was collected from Company CJD. Develop a pie chart that represents the data:

	Hand Injuries	Back Injuries	Leg Injuries
Number of Cases	13	36	4

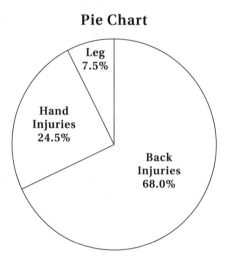

Pie Chart

6. The following data was collected from Company CJD. Develop a table that represents the data:

Group	Production	Quality Assurance	Maintenance
	Male	Male	Male
	Female	Female	Female
	Male	Male	Male
	Female	Male	Male
	Male	Male	Male
	Female	Male	Female
	Male	Female	Male
	Female	Male	Male
	Male	Male	Male
	Male	Male	Female

Sample Table

Table XX. Frequency of Cases by Gender of the Subject and Department [a]

	Production	Quality Assurance	Maintenance	Total
Male	6	8	7	21
Female	4	2	3	9
Total	10	10	10	30

[a]*All cases from CJD Incorporated.*

7. What type of data are bar charts typically used to represent?

   Bar charts use frequency data collected by categories.

8. What type of data is a line chart typically used to represent?

   Line charts use continuous data broken down by groups and collected over a period of time that is also measured as a continuous variable.

9. When developing a table to present data, what are some general guidelines for developing the table?

   - *Tables should be simple. Two or three tables are preferred to one large table.*
   - *Tables should be self-explanatory.*
   - *The title should be clear and concise, to the point. It answers the questions of what, when, and where.*
   - *Each row and column should be labeled clearly and concisely. The specific units for the data measured should be given. Columns should be separated with a vertical line.*
   - *Row and column totals should be shown.*
   - *Codes, abbreviations, or symbols should be explained in detail in a footnote.*

10. When developing a line chart to present data, what are some general guidelines for developing the chart?

    Each line represents a different group, while the points on the lines represent the obtained values for each measurement period. The horizontal axis represents a continuous variable, such as time, and the vertical axis represents the frequency data. When constructing the line chart, each line should be distinct from one another and a legend should indicate what each line represents.

Chapter 7

1. Provide three examples of benefits that effective leadership can provide a safety metrics program:

    Developing effective leadership can provide such benefits as:

    - *managers at all levels providing a more strategic approach to planning improvements;*
    - *managers increasing their ability to overcome resistance and encourage the wholehearted involvement of people in continual improvement activities;*
    - *employees contributing their energy and commitment more willingly to the aims of the organization;*
    - *individuals improving their performance when working in teams and project groups;*
    - *better relationships between customers, suppliers and people in other departments.*

2. Describe three activities leaders should focus an organization on:

    - *enabling everyone in the enterprise to develop a shared vision of the future and planning how to achieve it;*
    - *developing a culture of innovation and continual improvement towards all products and processes;*
    - *taking positive action to enable everyone at all levels to contribute their full potential towards the vision and their own work.*

3. Describe the four parts of accountability:

    Accountability consists of four parts: Identify a person(s), set an agreed upon time, establish milestone(s) and a formal system.

4. Define collaboration:

    Collaboration is the working together by people, departments and organizations from different backgrounds to meet a common goal.

5. What are the basic requirements of the data used in a performance program?

    Basic requirements for performance data include data that is identified, attainable and related back to the overall program goals and objectives.

6. Provide some examples of resources that can be used to collect information pertaining to safety performance:

    Some of the traditional resources include accident records, insurance claims, first aid reports, OSHA records, etc.

7. Describe some major downfalls to a safety performance program with regards to data:

   A major downfall for a metrics program is relying upon data that is not easily obtainable or trying to improve program performance using data that is not valid or reliable. The data collected also may not be linked to safety performance.

8. Characteristics of ideal data that can be used in a safety performance program include:

   Data should be valid, reliable and easily obtainable.

9. Describe four different types of measurement systems:

   - *Direct measurement systems are usually used when there is a unit of production or an event that is captured in an automated system such as a computer.*
   - *Indirect measurement systems are used when the actual data is not collected at the time the event occurs.*
   - *Statistical samples can be used to develop estimates where whole data is incomplete.*
   - *Interviews or surveys to gather metric information are used as a last resort.*

10. Describe the overall framework for a safety metrics program:

    A safety metrics program consists of identifying the goals and objectives of the organization. Data needs are identified and measurements that can be used to determine the status of the organization, then comparisons are made against a benchmark. If gaps are identified, follow-up action can be implemented.

Chapter 8

1. Define the term "benchmarking":

   Benchmarking, the planned, deliberate process of seeking out and targeting competitive continuous improvement by emulating industry's "best practices."

2. What functions does benchmarking serve for an organization?

   Benchmarking serves as a measuring stick for the organization by identifying those organizations that are viewed as the best.

3. An optimum benchmark can be characterized by what qualities?

   - *The benchmark should be measurable in terms of cost, time, value or some other quantitative parameter.*
   - *The benchmark should be meaningful and relevant.*
   - *Benchmarks that use simple productivity measures are often the best and often the most easily accessible.*
   - *The benchmarks should be available in external and competitive environments.*

4. Differentiate between internal benchmarking, functional benchmarking, competitive benchmarking and generic benchmarking:

   - *Internal benchmarking is done within an organization and typically between closely related divisions, similar plants or operations, or equivalent business units, using common or shared performance parameters as a basis for comparison*
   - *Functional benchmarking is a comparison of performance and procedures between similar business functions, but in different organizations and industries.*
   - *Competitive benchmarking generally focuses on direct competitors within the same industry and with specific comparable business operations.*
   - *Generic benchmarking is undertaken with external companies in different industries, which represent the "best-in-class" for particular aspects of the selected business operations.*

5. Describe the six steps in the benchmarking process:

   They are surveying, identification, prioritization, developing a plan, implementing a plan, and follow-up.

6. Describe the "continuous improvement process:"

   Continuous improvement process involves establishing performance measures, performing, measuring, identifying gaps, and improving.

7. Describe the PDCA management cycle:

   The PDCS management cycle is the classic plan-do-check-act (PDCA) cycle.

8. Describe some disadvantages to benchmarking:

   - *The senior management of an organization may be unsure of the concept or reluctant to admit that their competitors or other organizations may be more effective than their own.*
   - *Senior management has a natural tendency to look for quick results, but in best practices benchmarking there will almost certainly be disappointments and failures en route.*

9. Describe the five-step benchmarking process used by Motorola Corporation:

   1. The topics that are to be benchmarked are identified.
   2. The approach to be used for gathering data is determined.
   3. Benchmarking partners are identified.
   4. The benchmarking partner's approach is carefully studied.
   5. An action plan is created.

Chapter 9

1. Describe the purpose of the auditing process in a safety performance measurement program:

    The common purpose of auditing and inspecting is to find and eliminate hazards.

2. Describe three areas that audits can be used to obtain data for a safety metrics program:

    An audit or inspection is the monitoring function conducted in an industrial organization to locate and report existing and potential hazards, or man-environment systems or conditions, that have the capacity to cause accidents or illnesses in the workplace. Another key use for the safety audits is the collection of data and information to determine if the safety performance is meeting the desired goals and benchmarks.

3. Describe three purposes an audit can serve for an organization:

    1. reduce injury and illness rates

    2. do the "right thing"

    3. be in compliance with OSHA regulations

4. Differentiate between a planned and a continuous audit:

    Planned audits are conducted periodically at a preplanned date and time. Continuous audits are conducted on a frequent regular basis.

5. For an audit program, describe some personnel factors one should address when implementing such a program:

    Use trained personnel, provide personnel with an audit instrument and a formal audit procedure.

6. Describe some characteristics a good audit instrument should follow:

    Audits should have instructions or procedures for their completion. Items should be evaluated in terms of validity and reliability.

7. Differentiate between the validity of an audit instrument and its reliability:

    Validity means is the instrument measuring what it is supposed to measure. Reliable means does the instrument provide consistent information.

8. Describe some problems that can arise if the audit is not properly linked to the organization's performance:

    The audit can provide the users wrong information about the safety program and direct activity to wrong areas.

9. Describe the importance that follow-up action has in the audit process:

    One purpose of the audit is to identify deficiencies. The deficiencies need to be corrected once they have been identified. The follow-up is key to success of the audit program.

10. What are some benefits and problems with audits and the audit process?
    - *Can be construed as faultfinding*
    - *May produce only a superficial laundry list*
    - *May produce no remedial actions*
    - *May produce only inadequate remedial action*
    - *Benefits include providing a source of safety performance information, identifying deficiencies for correcting them.*

Chapter 10

1. What does an experience modification factor represent?

    The experience rating modification factor attempts to reflect an insured's actual losses in relation to the same insured's premium.

2. What importance do insurance costs have with respect to a safety metrics program?

    Insurance costs have been shown to be an objective measure for safety program performance.

3. Describe three categories of insurance expenses that can be monitored?

    Three categories of insurance expenses include incurred expenses, expense ratios, and combined expense ratios.

4. Company A had an EMR of .75 while Company B had an EMR of 2.7. Assuming they are the same industries with like types of employment, what conclusions can be drawn?

    Company A was paying a workers' compensation premium that was less than the expected amount for like types of companies in the same industry. Company B on the other hand was paying a workers' compensation premium that was over two and one half times greater than the expected premium for the same type of industry.

5. What is an expense ratio?

    The expenses are costs to the insured in excess of the losses.

6. What importance do combined ratios have?

    The expense ratio plus the loss ratio equals the "combined ratio." The combined ratio indicates the amount taken in by an insurance company versus the amount paid out.

7. What factors can contribute to raising an organization's EMR?

   Examples include the frequency of losses, amount of losses, payroll dollars, and class codes.

8. Describe three programs that can be implemented to control an organization's EMR:

   Loss control programs designed to control the frequency of claims, audit programs to ensure losses are properly recorded and closed out, and self insurance of smaller claims to reduce the frequency of claims paid by the insurance company.

9. What is a manual premium?

   The manual premium is developed by multiplying a published workers' compensation employee classification rate by each $100 of payroll for that employee classification.

10. What organization may determine a company's EMR?

   NCCI or other authorized insurance rating organization.

Chapter 11

1. What does the term Behavior-Based Safety mean?

   Behavior-Based Safety refers to a process designed to reduce the frequency of work-related accidents by first reducing the frequency of negative or inappropriate employee behaviors.

2. Describe the process of Behavior-Based Safety:

   A traditional Behavior-Based Safety process identifies critical behavior, then establishes management processes that reinforce positive behaviors.

3. What are some examples as to what may influence behaviors in the self directed stage?

   Examples of motivators are those that will elicit a positive response.

4. What is the goal of BBS?

   The goal is to educate employees and institute processes that involve them in behavioral analysis, observation, and correction.

5. What is the primary objective of a BBS program?

   The primary objective of measuring safety performance is to provide a feedback mechanism that will foster continuous improvement.

6. Define "critical behavior."

   Critical behaviors are those behaviors that have been identified as being critical to safety performance in the workplace.

7. What are some characteristics of a successful BBS program?

    Successful BBS programs use a process blueprint, emphasize communication, demonstrate leadership, ensure team competence, use action-oriented training, use data to ensure continuous improvement and provide technical resources.

8. How would one go about identifying critical behaviors in an organization?

    These behaviors can be identified using one of four different sources; incident reports, employee interviews, job observations and review of work rules and procedure manuals.

9. What is the strongest reinforcer for a behavior?

    Positive reinforcement of wanted behaviors increases the likelihood that the behavior will be performed again. Motivational interventions include positive incentive or rewards for targeted behaviors.

10. Differentiate between an incentive and a deterrent:

    Incentives are rewards that promote wanted behaviors while deterrents are negative reinforcers that punish unwanted behaviors.

Chapter 12

1. Describe three different types of measures that can be used to assess safety training:

    Different types of measures include student reaction reflects receptiveness to the training, behavioral measure focusing on the actual transfer of knowledge gained for the workplace and results measure that assess productivity gain.

2. What are some useful purposes for evaluating safety training?

    Useful purposes include providing a basis for decisions and policymaking, assessing participant achievement, evaluating training program content and improving training materials and programs.

3. Distinguish between formative and summative evaluation:

    Formative evaluations are conducted during the operation of a program to provide program directors evaluative information useful in improving the program. Summative evaluation is conducted at the end of the program to provide potential consumers with judgments about the programs worth or merit.

4. Distinguish between qualitative and quantitative evaluation:

    Qualitative evaluations are conducted in natural settings; utilizes the researcher as the chief "instrument" in both data-gathering and analysis; emphasizes "thick description," that is, obtaining "real," "rich," "deep," data which illuminate every-day patterns of action and meaning from the perspective of those being studied; tends to focus on social processes rather than primarily or exclusively on outcomes. Quantitative evaluation by contrast, generally focuses on the testing of specific hypotheses that are smaller parts of some larger theoretical perspective.

5. What is the process of designing an objectives oriented evaluation process?

   In the objectives oriented evaluation approach, the purposes of some educational activity are specified, and the evaluation process focuses on the extent to which the objectives have been achieved.

6. Describe the process for evaluating web-based training programs:

   Web training should be subjected to the same forms of evaluation as are other types of training. Comprehensive evaluations of programs should include assessments of students' performance on specified outcomes, instructors' effectiveness, and the quality of courses and the program.

7. Provide an example that utilizes the UCLA model of evaluation:

   An example of using the UCLA model of evaluation for a safety-related situation is as follows:

   System Assessment: An evaluation is made with regards to the current level of safety performance in the workplace.

   Program Planning: Based upon the results of the assessment, those aspects of the safety performance that can be improved through safety training are identified. An evaluation is conducted to identify appropriate safety training programs.

   Program Implementation: The safety training programs are implemented. An evaluation is conducted to ascertain whether the programs have been introduced to the intended audiences and conducted in the intended manner.

   Program Improvement: Evaluations are conducted to determine whether the training programs are working and objectives are being met.

   Program Certification: The programs are evaluated with regards to their overall worth to the organization and potential for use for other safety problems in other facilities.

8. In order to improve the effectiveness of a training program, describe three areas that one would address:

   Examples of areas to address include: Did trainees learn the course content? Do they apply training on the job? Does the training make a difference?

9. Provide an example that utilizes the Tylerian Evaluation Approach:

    The Tylerian Evaluation Approach requires the following steps:
    Establish broad goals or objectives. Classify the goals or objectives. Define objec-
    tives in behavioral terms. Find situations in which achievement of objectives can
    be shown. Develop or select measurement techniques. Collect performance data.
    Compare performance data with behaviorally stated objectives.

Chapter 13

1. Describe the uses of perception surveys for the purpose of measuring safety per-
    formance:

    Perception surveys are used to measure attitudes toward and acceptance of safety
    and health programs.

2. How would one implement a safety performance measurement program that uti-
    lizes discrete observation?

    During discrete observation of employee performance, the employee must not be
    aware that his/her performance is being evaluated.

3. How can economic analysis be used to assess safety performance?

    Economic analysis transforms safety outcomes into tangible financial benefits to
    the organization. Economic benefits and losses can be monitored as a performance
    measure.

4. What is risk management and how can it be used in a safety performance assess-
    ment program?

    Risk management involves the measurement of financial returns from safety and
    loss control activities. Risk managers evaluate the costs of implementing safety
    program activities compared to their costs and the overall savings to the organi-
    zation in terms of decreased losses, lowered insurance costs.

5. In the methodology for cost benefit analysis, the first step is identifying stake-
    holders. How would one go about completing this step?

    Identifying those who are of concern relative to the investments being entertained.
    This might include those who will provide the resources that will enable a solu-
    tion, those who will create the solution, those who will implement the solution,
    and those who will benefit from the solution.

6. What is systems safety and how can it be used to assess safety performance?

    Systems safety is the analysis field that utilizes techniques for identifying poten-
    tial sources of accidents and losses. Various techniques can be used to assess safety
    performance with regards to equipment, people, the environment and processes.

7. Describe fault tree analysis and how the procedure can be used to assess safety performance:

   The Fault Tree Analysis procedure is a top down analysis procedure that identifies undesirable events and their contributing factors. Once a tree has been developed, probabilities of failures can be determined for individual components in the tree. With the individual probabilities, overall probabilities of failures can be calculated for event paths using Boolean algebra.

8. Describe root cause analysis and how the procedure can be used to assess safety performance:

   The purpose of the Root Cause Analysis is to identify causal factors relating to a mishap or near-miss incidents. The technique goes beyond the direct causes to identify fundamental reasons for the fault or failure.

9. What impact has the military had upon systems safety?

   Much of the systems safety techniques and management program development has its roots in the military. The MIL STD 882D, Systems Safety provides a detailed framework for implementing a systems safety program.

10. Describe the Balanced Scorecard management system and explain how it can be used to assess safety performance:

    The Balanced Scorecard methodology builds on some key concepts of previous management ideas such as Total Quality Management (TQM), including customer-defined quality, continuous improvement, employee empowerment, and primarily measurement-based management and feedback.

Chapter 14

1. The exposure number of 200,000 man-hours represents what in an OSHA incidence rate?

   The OSHA incidences rates are based upon 200,000 hours of exposure which is equivalent to a company with 100 employees each working 2,000 hours in a calendar year. This corresponds to what an "average" full-time employee would work in a 40-hour week during a 52-week year (minus two weeks for vacation and holidays).

2. What purpose do rates serve?

   Rates allow for an "apples to apples" comparison between two or more groups.

3. A company experienced 15 OSHA recordable injuries over a year. The organization accumulated 1,220,000 man-hours. What is the OSHA recordable injury rate?

   2.46 recordable injuries per 200,000 man-hours.

4. When calculating penalties, OSHA may reduce the penalty because of what factors?

   The penalties may be reduced based upon the size of the business, the good faith of the employer and the employer's history of previous violations.

5. What role does the Census of Fatal Occupational Injuries play in national statistics?

   A comprehensive source for data concerning occupational fatalities is maintained by the Bureau of Labor Statistics' (BLS) Census of Fatal Occupational Injuries (CFOI).

6. How is the DOE's ratio of lost workdays to lost workday cases calculated?

$$Ratio\ of\ Lost\ Workdays\ to\ Lost\ Workday\ Cases = \frac{\#\ Lost\ Workdays}{\#\ Lost\ Workday\ Cases}$$

7. What does the DOE's Cost Index approximate?

   The index is approximately equal to the cents lost per hour worked.

8. What is the MIL STD 882D?

   MIL STD 882D is the current version of the System Safety Program requirements.

Chapter 15

1. What does VPP represent?

   OSHA's VPP criteria are a model; they are available to all companies-any size, any industry, and any location that serve as a framework for a comprehensive safety program.

2. Describe the benefits of cooperating with OSHA in the VPP program:

   Cooperative interaction with OSHA gives companies the opportunity to provide OSHA with input on safety and health matters and to provide industry with models of effective means for accomplishing workplace safety and health objectives.

3. Describe some of the benefits of participating in OSHA's VPP program:

   Participants are not subject to routine OSHA inspections, because OSHA's VPP onsite reviews ensure that their safety and health programs provide superior protection. Establishing and maintaining safety and health programs on the VPP model are reflected in substantially lower than average worker injury rates at VPP worksites. While protecting workers from occupational safety and health hazards, companies following the management guidelines mandated for VPP membership also experience decreased costs in workmen's compensation and lost work time, and often experience increased production and improved employee morale.

4. Describe the components of a safety program that would indicate management leadership and involvement:

   Management demonstrates commitment to safety and health protection by establishing policies and results-oriented objectives for worker safety, establishing goals for the safety and health programs and objectives for meeting that goal, communicating goals and objectives and integrating authority and responsibility for safety and health.

5. How can OSHA's VPP program criteria be used to improve safety performance?

   OSHA's VPP criteria can be used as a framework companies can strive toward meeting when developing and implementing a comprehensive safety program.

6. Describe the process of participating in OSHA's VPP program:

   In the VPP, management, labor, and OSHA establish a cooperative relationship at a workplace that has implemented a strong program:

   - *Management agrees to operate an effective program that meets an established set of criteria.*

   - *Employees agree to participate in the program and work with management to assure a safe and healthful workplace.*

   - *OSHA initially verifies that the program meets the VPP criteria. We then publicly recognize the site's exemplary program, and remove the site from routine scheduled inspection lists (OSHA may still investigate major accidents, valid formal employee complaints, and chemical spills).*

   - *OSHA also reassesses periodically to confirm that the site continues to meet VPP criteria (every three years for the Star program; every year for the merit program).*

7. Describe the components of a safety program that would indicate line accountability:

   Demonstration of a system for holding managers, supervisors, and employees accountable, defined authority and responsibility for safety and health.

8. Describe five areas that would be evaluated during the worksite analysis of the VPP program:

   Planning and integration of safety, job monitoring systems, hazard analysis systems, site inspections programs with follow-up, hazard recognition training, employee hazard reporting system and follow-up, written accident/incident investigation reporting system in place with follow-up, system to analyze: injury and illness trends over time through a review of injury/illness experience hazards identified through inspections, employee reports, and accident investigations, prior OSHA complaint inspections or informal complaints.

9. What provisions for contract workers should be made?

    Written safety program covering contract workers, written program providing for control of safety and health conditions for other contractors and subcontractor employees, communication methods for contract workers.

10. Describe the components of a safety program that would indicate acceptable safety and health training:

    Appropriate training being provided, employees understand hazards and their roles in protecting themselves, supervisors understand their role in assuring that employees understand and follow protective rules, managers understand their safety and health responsibilities.

11. Differentiate between national consensus standards and voluntary standards:

    National consensus standards are developed though a process of soliciting input from interested parties in the development and adoption of the standards. Voluntary standards are standards that are not enforceable by a party. National consensus standards unless adopted by an enforcing body as law, are not enforceable.

12. Describe the American National Standards Institute's role in developing consensus standards:

    The American National Standards Institute (ANSI) promotes the use of U.S. standards internationally, advocates U.S. policy and technical positions in international and regional standards organizations, and encourages the adoption of international standards as national standards where these meet the needs of the user community.

Index